THE STORY OF

Maserati

Text and design copyright © 2025 Headline Publishing Group Limited

First published in 2025 by Welbeck
An Imprint of HEADLINE PUBLISHING GROUP

1

Cataloguing in Publication Data is available from the British Library

Hardback ISBN 978-1-03542-394-1

Printed and bound in China

HEADLINE PUBLISHING GROUP LIMITED
An Hachette UK Company
Carmelite House
50 Victoria Embankment
London EC4Y 0DZ

The authorised representative in the EEA is Hachette Ireland,
8 Castlecourt Centre, Dublin 15, D15 XTP3, Ireland (email: info@hbgi.ie)

www.headline.co.uk
www.hachette.co.uk

THE STORY OF

A TRIBUTE TO
AUTOMOTIVE EXCELLENCE

STUART CODLING

WELBECK

Contents

House of the Trident

Seven Brothers

An age-old maxim has it that you can choose your friends
but you cannot choose your family. In over 100 years the
Maserati company has passed through several different
ownerships but it owes its stature, if not its continued
existence, to the shared engineering passion of brothers
for whom a delight in all things mechanical far outweighed
any nagging sibling rivalries.

The first son born to Rodolfo Maserati and Carolina Losi arrived
in 1881, a febrile time in Italian history. The country as we
know it today was just 20 years old, following a consolidation
of various states – some previously occupied by Austrian forces –
into one kingdom ruled by Victor Emmanuel II. This energetic
young nation was already making and breaking friendships
with its neighbours as it eyed foreign expansion. Already it had
captured more territory in further armed conflict with Austria,
annexed the Papal States and ended the temporal power of the
Holy See – and begun quarrelling with France, previously a key
ally against the enemy to the north-east.

OPPOSITE: Isotta Fraschini entered Alfieri Maserati in the 1908 Grand Prix
des Voiturettes in Dieppe.

Unification also drove the expansion of Italy's railways, a vitally important travel and communications network in this era before the invention of the motor car. Rodolfo worked on the railways – accounts differ as to whether he was a driver or a station master – and, shortly after his marriage to Carolina, moved from his native Piacenza to Voghera, an important junction between the Alessandria–Piacenza line and a recently completed line from Milan, the industrial and commercial engine of the north. His sons were captivated by the spectacle and noise of the mighty steam locomotives as they powered Italy towards its future.

Only six of the seven children born to Rodolfo and Carolina would live to adulthood. Carlo, the first, was joined by Bindo in 1883. Two years later a third son was supposedly to have been christened Alfiero, but a mistake on the registrar's part enshrined him in the records as Alfieri. This child lived a little over a year and the cause of his death remains unknown, such was the inexact nature of record-keeping at the time; when a fourth son came along, in September 1887, he was given the same name. Mario, the only son not to pursue a career in engineering, was born in 1890, followed by Ettore and Ernesto in 1894 and 1898.

Carlo was the ball of energy who gave his siblings leadership. As a pre-teen he began to build models of steam-powered cars. By the time Ernesto was born, Carlo was working in a bicycle factory – and had secured funding from a wealthy nobleman, the Marquis Carcano di Anzano del Parco, to develop and productionise a one-cylinder engine which could power a bicycle.

Between the births of the first and last of the Maserati brothers, Italy lurched into domestic ferment. Well-intentioned grain tariffs introduced to protect native farmers drove up food prices and provoked unrest, as did sundry political and

ABOVE: Alfieri Maserati at the wheel of a Diatto 4DC during the 1922 Italian Grand Prix weekend. Just three cars finished the arduous race on Monza's combined road course and oval.

financial corruption scandals and failures of the country's colonial ventures. Strikes and land occupations brought military intervention and, for a brief period, prime minister Francesco Crispi attempted to govern without parliament. In response, citizens gravitated towards Marxist demagogues. Railway workers were among those to form anarcho-syndicalist trade unions and agitate, often violently, for better pay and conditions.

Such were the conditions in which the brothers grew up. Despite Italy's delicate economic state, Carlo raced his bicycles successfully enough to catch the eye of his contemporary, Vincenzo Lancia, formerly a book-keeper for a bicycle importer but now making his name as a racing driver for Fiat, where he also worked as a tester. Like Carlo, Lancia was a self-taught engineer with a passion for speed. After three years working as a test driver with Lancia at Fiat's works in Turin, Carlo joined the Milanese luxury car manufacturer Isotta Fraschini as a mechanic and test driver, securing employment there for younger brother Alfieri too.

Carlo had a restless temperament and soon moved on to the car and motorbike manufacturer Bianchi, where he would have an opportunity to race, while Alfieri elected to stay at Isotta Fraschini. But as a racing driver Carlo was less successful than he had been on two wheels, finishing the 1907 Coppa Florio a distant ninth, 38 minutes behind the Isotta Fraschini of winner Ferdinando Minoia. Alfieri would enjoy a better result as a riding mechanic in the following year's event, partnering Vincenzo Trucco to second place. Shortly afterwards Carlo joined the recently merged Junior Automobiles/OTAV as general director and, while the company was on a downward trajectory, ceasing production by 1910, Carlo recruited brothers Bindo and Ettore and the three of them successfully designed a small aircraft.

Tragedy struck in 1910 as Carlo, having left to set up his own engineering consultancy with 15-year-old Ettore, succumbed to tuberculosis, the highly infectious lung condition which was the scourge of the urban working class. He was just 29 years old.

The brothers had lost their north star but, in Carlo's absence, Alfieri became the alpha male of the siblings. In common with his big brother he had an extrovert nature and a penchant for motor racing, though he was less impulsive. In staying at Isotta Fraschini while Carlo jumped from one employ to another, Alfieri had picked up a broader base of skills, becoming Cesare Isotta's mechanic and test driver, then assisting in sales and marketing as well as participating in the company's racing activities. In moving up the ranks – to the extent that he was trusted with overseas sales missions which took him as far as the Americas – Alfieri developed an understanding of the complete business.

Returning to Italy in 1913, Alfieri was tasked with opening a new sales and service centre in Bologna. While there an idea took root: opening his own business in partnership with his brothers. In December the following year they made it happen. While Bindo elected to remain with Isotta Fraschini, Ernesto and Ettore joined Alfieri in opening a garage on the Via de Pepoli, a tiny alley off the Piazza Santo Stefano. Paperwork lodged with the local chamber of commerce enshrined this enterprise as the *Società Anonima Officine Alfieri Maserati*, describing the purpose of the business as "the repair of cars".

Within months of opening up, the brothers had to put the business on pause, as Italy became embroiled in what would be known (until the next pan-European conflict) as The Great War. Ernesto was the last to be called up – in 1916, when he turned 18. But while the war destroyed a whole generation of young people across Europe, Alfieri, Ettore and Ernesto escaped unscathed – indeed, Alfieri and Ettore's mechanical skills ensured they never saw action on the front line.

Alfieri was dispatched to Milan, where the Nagliati company built Hispano-Suiza 8Aa aircraft engines under licence. As a side enterprise after his military service he developed a new type of spark plug with more durable mica-based insulation, which he patented and went into business manufacturing in partnership with his old Isotta Fraschini colleague, Vincenzo Trucco. Ettore worked for Franco Tosi Meccanica, a diesel engine manufacturer which had been turned over to aircraft engine production for the war.

As well as destruction, armed conflict also acts as a spur to innovation. Come peacetime, the brothers were eager to exploit new business opportunities and soon moved out of the cramped Via de Pepoli garage, relocating to a former glass-blowing factory outside Bologna on the old Roman road connecting Milan with Rimini. Within months of taking out the lease in April 1919, Alfieri had consolidated the spark plug manufacturing operation into the new facility and moved his (now retired) parents into an apartment upstairs.

Still it would be some time before the Maserati brothers graduated from fixing and tuning cars to building them. The slow-burn journey arguably began with Alfieri's decision to return to racing in the spring of 1920 with a second-hand 3-litre car built before the war by SCAT, a company later absorbed into Fiat. Among his rivals was a young Enzo Ferrari. The car was not competitive enough for Alfieri's liking and, after a disappointing and brief dalliance with a second-hand Nesselsdorf, he built his own 'Tipo Speciale' based on an

BELOW: Alfieri Maserati and riding mechanic Guerino Bertocchi claimed the company's first class victory, eighth overall, in the 1926 Targa Florio road race.

ABOVE: Celebrated racer
Achille Varzi (centre)
joined Alfieri Maserati
(third from left) from
Alfa Romeo, winning the
Coppa Acerbo.

Isotta Fraschini chassis with an Hispano-Suiza engine and the
SCAT's gearbox.

Although the Tipo Speciale was fast enough for Alfieri
and Ernesto (acting as riding mechanic) to win the Susa-
Moncenisio hillclimb, in road races it was still outgunned and
for the 1922 racing season the Maseratis acquired an Isotta
Fraschini which they extensively modified in-house. Further
wins attracted the attention of Turin's Autocostruzioni Diatto,
the second-biggest car manufacturer in Italy, who offered
Alfieri and Ernesto positions as engineering consultants as well
as the opportunity to race.

While the deal was irresistible it was also short-lived, and an object lesson in the perils of post-war Italy's seesawing economy. The 4.5-litre Diatto 20S was often beaten by smaller, lighter rivals and Alfieri was rewarded for reverting to his Tipo Speciale with a third consecutive victory at Susa-Moncenisio in 1923. The following season he was handed a five-year ban from racing after it was discovered that his car for a hillclimb in Spain, entered as a 2-litre, had undergone an engine swap to a 3-litre the night before the event. Diatto's official history claims the company was innocent and Alfieri was the culprit, while Maserati chronicles say the opposite; whatever the truth of the matter, the ban was rescinded after a year and Diatto continued to employ the brothers.

When motor racing's governing body announced a manufacturers' world championship for grands prix in 1925, Diatto wanted to get involved – and commissioned the Maseratis to develop and build a new supercharged 2-litre, 8-cylinder engine. Development work dragged on, stymied by the death of illustrious test driver Onesimo Marchiso in an accident, and the car was only ready for the final race of the season at Monza in September. It broke down after 39 of the 80 laps with Emilio Materassi at the wheel. It became clear the company's ambition exceeded their finances – they blamed the government for being slow to pay monies owed from wartime – and Diatto grudgingly withdrew from motor racing.

Such was the Maserati brothers' reputation on the domestic and international racing scene by this point that one of Diatto's customers, the Marquis Diego de Sterlich Aliprandi, an Abruzzo aristocrat with a huge personal fortune, offered to buy the company's remaining racing inventory and transfer it to the Maseratis. The Marchese Volante, as he was known to the racing public, would become a pivotal figure in the Maserati company's transition from tuning shop to car manufacturer.

ABOVE: Maserati's first car was the Tipo 26, based on inventory acquired from the moribund Diatto marque with funding from Marquis Diego de Sterlich.

The ten ex-Diatto chassis and engines formed the basis of the first cars to carry the Maserati name and badge. For this, brother Mario – by then an established and successful artist – took the trident motif from the renaissance fountain of Neptune in the centre of Bologna.

For 1926 the world championship was expanded to five races and engine displacement capped at 1.5 litres – regular fiddling with the rules was one of the reasons the races were poorly supported by manufacturers – and the Maserati brothers adapted the ex-Diatto design to take advantage of this, downsizing the engine from two litres. Alfieri gave the first Maserati-badged car, the Tipo 26, its public race debut

in the Targa Florio road race around Sicily in April 1926.
As a non-championship event it was open to larger-engined
cars and Alfieri and his riding mechanic, Guerino Bertocchi,
finished eighth overall but top of the 1500cc class. Two months
later Ernesto took overall victory in the Chilometro Lanciato
(Flying Kilometre) race along the old Roman road in Bologna,
reaching nearly 104mph, and the order books began to fill.
In all, Maserati would build over 40 Tipo 26s to various
specifications for gentlemen racers.

Major challenges lay ahead, though. As a small business,
Maserati lacked economies of scale and it was difficult to turn
a profit. Time and again Alfieri would have to lean on the

generosity of Diego de Sterlich to keep his company afloat, and his health became a problem after he lost a kidney in an accident on the Coppa di Messina in 1927. The following year, racing's governing body of national automobile clubs gave up on the 1.5-litre formula – and, owing to continued lack of big-manufacturer interest, the world championship itself. That idea would lie fallow until 1950.

Maserati responded to the challenges of the racetrack and developed bigger engines despite lack of funds. Ingenuity would have to trump spend – Maserati's next grand prix car was powered by a four-litre V16 engine made by joining two of the existing two-litre straight-eights via a common crankcase. The company acquired such a reputation on track that no less an eminence than Tazio Nuvolari, the Flying Mantuan, turned to Maserati when he flounced out of Scuderia Ferrari in 1933.

Still the company was in crisis mode. Alfieri, for so long the driving force of Maserati, died in March 1933 after surgery to save his remaining kidney failed. The city of Bologna went into public mourning and businesses closed down for the day as his funeral cortege passed through. Nuvolari and Enzo Ferrari were among the well-known racers paying their respects.

Bindo Maserati left Isotta Fraschini to join his brothers, assuming the business reins while Ernesto took over technical direction. But despite further success on track, the company's income from sales and prizes barely matched its outgoings. Production slowed to a crawl as suppliers declined to provide raw materials for which they might not be paid. The Maseratis turned to Italy's national motoring club for loans and offered Piedmontese industrialist Gino Revere the presidency of the company in exchange for further investment.

Ultimately, though, commercial salvation would come from closer to home.

BELOW: Tension at the start of the 1934 Nice Grand Prix as Tazio Nuvolari (2) lines up his Maserati 8CM alongside Achille Varzi's Alfa Romeo P3 (28) and the Bugatti of René Dreyfus (20).

Move to Modena

Exit The Brothers

Shorn of Alfieri's entrepreneurial drive, the Maserati brothers
struggled against financial and competitive headwinds
through the 1930s. The Great Depression touched businesses
all over the world and, arguably, played a role in igniting the
populist tinderbox in Germany, where the newly elected
fascist government saw motor racing as an important
propaganda and national prestige tool.

Unable to compete on equal terms with state-backed enterprises
on track (*see* Chapter 3), Maserati built just nine cars in 1936
despite the backing of wealthy benefactors such as industrialist
and amateur racer Gino Rovere, one of the co-investors in the
Scuderia Subalpina team which acted as Maserati's 'works'
team in grands prix.

Salvation arrived via the Bolognese-based sports newspaper
Littoriale. To describe the remarkably well-connected Corrado
Filippini as a 'reporter' is to undersell the significance of an
individual who would later act as the company's formal entrant
in the Indianapolis 500 and broker the sale of many historically
significant Maserati race cars to the US after World War II.

OPPOSITE: Wilbur Shaw won two consecutive Indianapolis 500s in a Maserati 8CTF.

ABOVE: Adolfo Orsi
poses with a new
Quattroporte in 1963.
Commercial necessity
had driven him to begin
expanding the road car
range in the 1950s.

Aware of Maserati's predicament, Filippini brokered a meeting between the brothers and self-made Modenese businessman Adolfo Orsi, another of his acquaintances.

Born in March 1888, Orsi was one of nine siblings. His father was a rag-and-bone man and, after leaving school at the age of 11, Adolfo became a butcher's apprentice. This entailed early starts and a lunchtime finish; in the afternoon he would pull a cart around the areas not covered by his father, selling fruit and collecting rags. When his father died two years later the young Adolfo in effect took over the family business, acquiring more horses and carts and pressing his siblings into service as sorters of the scavenged items. Soon he was sending wagonloads of scrap metal to local foundries and eyeing up the possibility of going into the metal foundry business himself. By the mid-1930s the Orsi Group owned dozens of foundries and was expanding into other fields such as railways, agricultural machinery and automobile sales.

Although Orsi's lack of interest in motor racing rendered him an outlier among putative Maserati investors, Filippini sold him on the potential promotional value of racing to his existing businesses, plus the untapped potential of the spark plug business which had been drifting since Alfieri's death. On the weekend of 20–21 September 1936, the brothers made the short trip from Bologna for the non-championship Circuito de Modena races, where Ferdinando Barbieri was racing a 6C 34 against stronger Alfa Romeo machinery in a thin field of grand prix cars but Maseratis formed the majority of the field in a separate event for 'voiturettes'. In that, early Scuderia Ferrari investor Count Carlo Felice Trossi beat former motorcycle racer Clemente Biondetti (nicknamed 'The Wolf of Tuscany') in a battle of the 6CMs.

BELOW: The 6CM was competitive in the 'Voiturette' racing class and production accelerated after Adolfo Orsi bought Maserati in 1937.

In an Orsi-owned property adjoining the mechanical scrutineering area, the parties met – and quickly found common ground. On 1 May 1937 the obligatory paperwork was signed enshrining Orsi as owner of Officine Alfieri Maserati and Fabbrica Candele Maserati. The brothers' surname remained above the door, but they were now theoretically free agents. Ernesto, Ettore and Bindo agreed ten-year contracts as employees; Orsi assumed the commercial reins and installed his son, Omar, as managing director while the brothers focused on design, engineering and racing. Orsi also arranged for a new factory to be built at Modena to house the Maserati businesses, though it would not be ready until 1939.

In the interim, production accelerated immediately to 14 cars in 1937. And, though the company remained outgunned on the Grand Prix scene by the German government-backed

Mercedes and Auto Union, and challenged in the voiturette class by the new British ERA organization, a new opportunity beckoned.

In 1930 the organizers of the Indy 500, enticed by Maserati's burgeoning reputation on the European racing scene, had reached a tentative hand across the Atlantic. Then less than 20 years old, the event was still building towards its reputation as "the greatest spectacle in racing". European marques had made the journey and come away with victory several times in its first decade but had drifted away in the 1920s. That decade had been regarded as a golden era of competition at the 'Brickyard' but this did not prevent the new owners of the Indianapolis Motor Speedway, led by World War I fighter pilot Eddie Rickenbacker, from successfully lobbying the American Automobile Association to change its rules to accommodate "less expensive, less specialized" cars and broaden the scope of entries. They also substantially reduced the previously lucrative prize purse.

Derided as a "junk formula" to this day, the 1930–1937 Indy 500 technical package was interpreted as closing the door to European Grand Prix-type cars. The chief obstacles were the insistence on each car having a riding mechanic as well as a driver – a thoroughly outdated practice – and a ban on superchargers in four-stroke engines. Alfieri Maserati was interested enough to send one of his new 16-cylinder V4s to be driven by regular V4 racer Baconin Borzacchini, with Ernesto Maserati as riding mechanic. Textile magnate and amateur racer Letterio Cucinotta then filed an entry for his Maserati 26B. Running without superchargers, neither car was competitive in the race; Borzacchini, no doubt to the delight of the radio commentators struggling to wrap their tongues around his name, was forced out on lap seven with electrical problems. Cucinotta was still circulating an hour after eventual winner Billy Arnold had taken the chequered flag. After this low-key debut, Maserati would not return to the Brickyard for several years.

When the V8RIs proved unsuccessful in grand prix racing all four examples were sold into American hands. Steel magnate Henry Topping Jr – later famous for proposing to movie star Lana Turner by dropping a diamond ring into her martini – had his modified to accommodate a second seat and entered it in the 1937 Indy 500 as the 'Topping Special'. Despite the best efforts of experienced track racer Egbert 'Babe' Stapp, it scraped onto the grid 31st out of 33 and retired with clutch failure. But still there was a surge of interest among European marques for the Indy 500 and, more specifically, the financially lucrative Vanderbilt Cup. Further rule changes in the US (including the removal of the riding mechanic) and in European grand prix racing proved the spur to develop new cars and, by 1939, Maserati's new 8CTF was coming into its own, if still not a match for the German cars.

After the first two chassis demonstrated the 8CTF's potential on track in 1938, Maserati built a third and put out feelers to the USA. The buyer was a fascinating individual whose shady past and Chicago mob associations have caused him to be partially erased from motor racing history. Michael Boyle, known as 'Umbrella Mike' on account of his habit of collecting cash bribes in his umbrella, managed the International Brotherhood of Electrical Workers, Chicago's most powerful union. He also had a passion for the Indy 500 but, by 1939, his first win as a team owner was a receding memory and he had grown frustrated with the process of trying to wring more speed out of his existing cars. The 8CTF seemed like a perfect opportunity and his well-drilled crew prepared it beautifully, carefully tuning it to run on the methanol fuel used at Indy. With Wilbur Shaw at the wheel, the 'Boyle

Special' Maserati dominated the Indy 500 in 1939 and 1940, and would likely have won again in 1941 but for a wheel failure which put Shaw in the wall.

By this point Europe was in the grip of war again and the Maserati factories, along with other Orsi facilities, had been turned over to the maintenance of military vehicles and manufacture of electric wagons. The race cars were spirited away to avoid being melted down for munitions. As the US became enveloped in the conflict Rickenbacker closed Indianapolis Motor Speedway at the end of that year, cancelled the 1942 Indy 500, and announced there would be no more racing until after the war was over. By 1945 the predominantly wooden grandstands and pit buildings were rotting and the golf course Rickenbacker had installed on the infield was virtually a jungle. Local businessman Tony Hulman bought

ABOVE: With two wins, two third places and a fourth, the 'Boyle Special' Maserati 8CTF remains the most successful car to have raced in the Indianapolis 500.

ABOVE: The 1936
Imperial Trophy at
Crystal Palace was
notable not only for
Luigi Villoresi's entry
in a 6CM, but also for
being the first motor
race to be televised live.

the facility for $750,000 and installed Shaw as president
and general manager. Ted Horn finished third in the Boyle
Maserati in the first post-war Indy 500 of 1946, was third again
the following year, then fourth in 1948. The car's swansong
came in 1950, when future winner Bill Vukovich completed
his rookie orientation in it.

Despite this success in the US, and decent showings by
Maserati customers in European postwar races, as the brothers
came to the end of their ten-year contracts with Orsi in 1947
they began to weigh their futures. Ettore, Ernesto and Bindo
continued to live in Bologna and commuted by train or
bicycle to Modena. They had no problem with Orsi, though
it is also widely claimed that they had felt undermined by
the appointment in 1940 of Alberto Massimino as technical
director. Massimino, a longtime employee of Fiat and Alfa
Romeo, was among the engineers who had 'left' Alfa along

with Enzo Ferrari during the corporate bloodletting of 1937, and worked with Enzo on the 'secret' Auto Avio Costruzione 815 racer which preceded the birth of the Ferrari car company. If Massimino's recruitment was a problem, it did not prevent Ernesto from collaborating with him on a clandestine road car project kept secret from the Italian and German regimes.

Based on the 6CM race car, the A6 ('A' for Alfieri Maserati, six being the number of cylinders in the engine) was a neat sports-coupé designed by Battista 'Pinin' Farina, founder of the famous coachworking company, powered by a 1.5-litre inline six-cylinder engine producing 65bhp. Some elements of the prototype shown at the Geneva Motor Show in March 1947, including the retractable headlamps, were removed, and production cars featured more window area. The coveted Grand Prix d'Elegance prize at Monte Carlo followed, as did a steady parade of potential customers. Maserati was now a manufacturer of road as well as race cars.

BELOW: Shortly before leaving, Ernesto Maserati co-developed the A6, Maserati's first road car. Early versions had a radiator grille shaped like a race car's; the 'Extra Lusso' models featured a wider one.

ABOVE: Despite tough financial circumstances, Maserati launched the 3500 GT in 1957, and it was an instant hit. Customers included crowned heads such as Prince Rainier of Monaco as well as Hollywood royalty such as Elizabeth Taylor and Rock Hudson.

Nevertheless the brothers decided to strike out on their own, setting up shop in Bologna in May 1947 as OSCA (Officine Specializzate Costruzione Automobili). The connection between the Maserati companies and the brothers who had founded them was terminated.

Adolfo Orsi had a sound commercial brain and knew how to run a business but his operations would be sorely tested by political and social unrest in the years to come. Tensions which had been building in Italy during wartime between those who supported the now-deposed fascist regime and those who covertly fought it erupted into ugly bouts of score-settling. As one who had been seen to have profited from the conflict, Orsi was in the firing line as Communists became increasingly influential in the politics of the region. While Maserati was less affected than some of his other businesses by industrial unrest, the general election of April 1948 created a flash point.

Within a year, relations between Orsi and various trade unions had declined to the point where he closed his car and spark plug factories for three months. While this brought some unions back to the negotiating table, the rancour metastasized to Orsi's iron and steel foundries, which he also closed down after a series of wildcat strikes. His refusal to re-hire known Communist agitators precipitated a borderline riot outside one foundry on 9 January 1950. Police opened fire, killing six people and injuring dozens more.

Orsi also faced internal divisions within his own family as his siblings took advantage of his diminished stature. Forced to split the empire up among his sisters and brother in 1953, Adolfo elected to keep the Maserati factory and the machine tool operation. In an initial burst of investment he employed the renowned race car designer Gioacchino Colombo, racer-engineer Vittorio Bellentani, and the promising young

ABOVE: Styled by Pietro Frua, the 1963 Quattroporte's discreet appearance belied the power (260bhp) of the race-based V8 under its bonnet.

Innocenti engineer Giulio Alfieri. In terms of quality of engineering, what followed is widely held to be a golden period for the company as the 250F racing car contributed to two world championships for Juan Manuel Fangio, the Tipo 60/61 'Birdcage' showcased clever lightweighting techniques in sportscar racing, and the Quattroporte and 3500 GT road cars entranced buyers as rarefied as the Shah of Persia.

And yet financial troubles always lurked in the margins. A lucrative machine tool contract with the Argentinian state went south when President Juan Perón was deposed in 1955, leaving Orsi at the mercy of the banks who had funded the raw-material purchases. Despite selling the machine-tool operation to a Swiss company and closing Maserati's in-house racing team, Orsi was unable to stave off his creditors and in 1958 Credito Italiano demanded the company be put into administration.

The road to solvency required the company to focus on road cars through the 1960s, but even Maserati's end of this industry was changing. To build and sell enough cars at a sufficiently accessible price to turn a consistent profit, it would be necessary to step back from the artisan-construction approach. Come the end of the decade, even Ferrari would capitulate to the realities of mass production.

In 1968, with an offer on the table from Argentinian entrepreneur Alejandro de Tomaso, Adolfo Orsi – perhaps mindful of how his dealings with that country had brought near-ruin a decade earlier – accepted an alternative proposal from French car marker Citroën. The deal would leave him with 40 per cent of the company, a clear voice in its future direction, and jobs in the Modenese factory safe. Or so he thought.

BELOW: In the late 1950s Omar Orsi asked for a more dynamic version of the 3500 GT and prolific stylist Giovanni Michelotti – then working for Vignale – obliged with the Sebring. The Series II model is distinguished by its side vents and chromed headlight surrounds.

Grand Prix

Born on Track

Like Ferrari, the Maserati legend was forged in the heat
of competition. And while Alfieri and Ernesto Maserati,
like Enzo Ferrari, were successful racing drivers in their
own right, the brothers were competing in cars they
had actually built themselves...

Long before 'the auto-car' supplanted the horse and cart as
the essential mode of long-distance transport for the masses,
people began to race this new invention. Alfieri Maserati
was born just over a year after Carl Benz demonstrated his
Patent Motorwagen on the streets of Mannheim; just before
Alfieri's seventh birthday in 1894 the first competitive event
for this genre of vehicle was held, the Paris to Rouen Horseless
Carriages contest. But this was hardly the kind of wheel-to-
wheel spectacle you might expect: since the nascent motor
industry had the common agenda of proving the reliability and
usefulness of its products, these early races tended to be point-
to-point trials of durability rather than performance.

Grand Prix ('great prize'), already a familiar term in
horse racing, definitively entered the motorsport lexicon
with the 1906 Grand Prix de l'ACF (Automobile Club de

OPPOSITE: Maserati's A6GCM Formula 2 car was based on the 4CLT 'Voiturette'.

BELOW: Henken Widengren contested the 1931 Ards TT in this Maserati with a supercharged 1100cc engine. Heavily modified by subsequent owner John Appleton and raced as the 'Appleton Special', it has been restored to 26M spec by the Mazjub family.

France). While the format was familiar – a time trial held on a triangular course of public roads, with two sessions on separate days – the winning prize of FF45,000 was unprecedented. National car clubs were taking the first steps down the road to promoting harmonious international competition by forming the *Association Internationale des Automobile Clubs Reconnus* (AIACR, later to become the FIA). By the 1920s the racing scene had matured to a point where the AIACR's sporting committee was framing a uniform technical formula that would enable it to run a world championship.

While this first attempt would founder after three years, a change to allow 1.5-litre supercharged cars facilitated Maserati's Grand Prix debut in 1926 with the Diatto-based Tipo 26. While the brothers continued to build larger-engined

variants for road-racing competions such as the Targa Florio, and smaller-engined cars for customers in less rarefied national events, the allure of racing for the biggest prize purses of all was irresistible. But the key challenge was a rulebook seemingly in constant flux; having abandoned the world championship concept after 1927 and embraced a laissez-faire approach at Grand Prix level, the AIACR realized that the so-called Formula Libre ('free formula') muddied the waters of what top-level racing should be.

An open rulebook also threatened to hand the competitive edge to the richest competitors, but Maserati's low-budget, high-ingenuity response showed how it was possible to do more with less. The V4 might have been hobbled by rule changes at Indianapolis, and come up short against the likes of Alfa Romeo in Europe, but the sheer audacity of mating two inline-eights to create a four-litre V16 deserves respect – even more so because it worked. This despite a plethora of vulnerable moving parts and friction surfaces: 32 valves, two crankshafts, four camshafts, two water pumps, four oil pumps and two superchargers.

The V4's significance in motor racing history goes beyond its modest success at Grand Prix level. On 28 September 1929, Baconin Borzacchini gunned the prototype V4 along the old state highway outside Cremona at an average of 152.93mph over two timed runs, a new ten-mile world speed record. Later the Bolognese automobile club held a gala dinner for Borzacchini and the Maserati brothers to celebrate this magnificent achievement. Also in attendance was Enzo Ferrari, working the room for potential clients for the racing team he had in mind: he encountered Alfredo Caniato and Mario Tadini, amateur racers and heirs to successful textile businesses. A month later Scuderia Ferrari was incorporated, with them as key investors.

In 1929 the AIACR had tried to curb increasing car speeds by introducing a fuel consumption formula. Combined with the financial crash of later that year, this had the effect of driving away competitors rather than encouraging them. But, amid a hotch-potch of cancelled races and occasionally thin fields, a fascinating battle of the Italian greats played out: Tazio Nuvolari in a Scuderia Ferrari-run Alfa Romeo P2 vs Achille Varzi, predominantly in Maserati's new 8C 26M. Bugatti Type 35s did most of the winning at Grand Prix level but it was the contest between the flamboyant Nuvolari (credited by Ferrari as inventing the four-wheel drift method of cornering) and the clinical, calculating Varzi which captured the imagination of racing fans at home and abroad. Sadly, having captured Maserati's first Grand Prix victory, in Spain in October, Varzi

then decided Bugatti would offer him a better opportunity for 1931; later in the decade his career would come unravelled as he developed an addiction to morphine.

The AIACR tinkered further with the rules as it tried to reboot the championship idea as a European competition, announcing a new formula coming in 1934 based around a maximum car weight of 750kg. Alfieri's last projects before he died were the V5 – a five-litre version of the V4 – and a new 8C model based around an inline-eight enlarged to three litres and, with an eye on cutting a cleaner path through the air, mounted in a noticeably narrower chassis than rivals. Making its debut at the 1933 Tunis Grand Prix, the definitive 8CM-3000 single-seater flexed so much that it alarmed spectators as well as drivers. In this era chassis structure continued to

BELOW: Based on the
26M chassis but with
a larger version of the
six-cylinder engine, the
8C 2800 of 1931 was an
interim step as Alfieri
Maserati worked towards
a three-litre engine.

follow the ancient practice of twin horizontal beams with
cross-bracing and a body fixed on top; in the 8CM-3000's case
the gap of just 50cm between the beams exacerbated a natural
tendency to flex.

Nevertheless Maserati was well placed to succeed against
Alfa Romeo, which was in the grip of financial crisis in
1933 and withdrew its new P2s from competition, leaving
Scuderia Ferrari to field lesser models until later in the year,
when Alfa was rescued by the fascist government's *Istituto
per la Ricostruzione Industriale* investment programme. One
consequence of this was Nuvolari temporarily severing his
ties with Enzo Ferrari after a series of mechanical failures had
eliminated him from race-winning positions. Matters came
to a head shortly before the Belgian Grand Prix, when news
emerged that Nuvolari would try a Maserati as well as his
regular Ferrari-prepared Alfa Romeo.

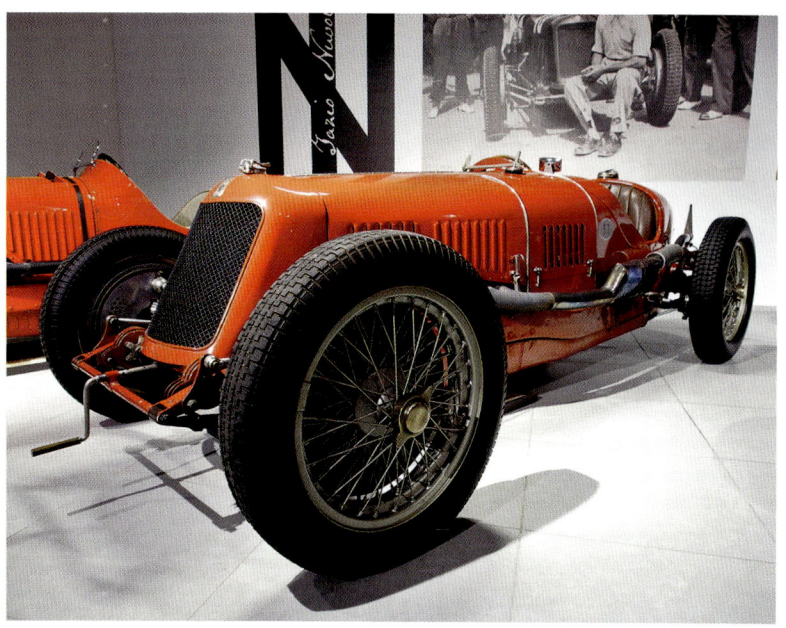

As it happened, there was an 8CM-3000 available: the first customer chassis, returned to the factory by Raymond Sommer after a disappointing Monaco Grand Prix. Despite Sommer's misgivings, Giuseppe Campari – a burly 41-year-old who planned to retire from racing and become a full-time opera singer at the end of the season – had demonstrated Maserati's competitiveness by winning the French Grand Prix in an 8C 26M before sustaining an eye injury at Reims. The morning after that race, Enzo Ferrari grudgingly reached an arrangement with Ernesto Maserati for the ex-Sommer 8CM-3000 to be entered by Scuderia Ferrari for Nuvolari in Belgium.

Even in the 21st century, Spa-Francorchamps is a stern test of skill and bravery. In 1933 its layout was over double

ABOVE: Tazio Nuvolari's
win for Maserati in
Nice in August 1933,
following victories in Spa
and Livorno, prompted
Alfa Romeo to make its
Tipo B cars available to
Scuderia Ferrari again.

the length and consisted entirely of public roads. Practice
convinced Nuvolari that the Maserati's bigger engine would
be an advantage if he could cure its alarming handling.
Accompanied by two mechanics, he took it to the Imperia
car factory in Nessonvaux, just outside Liège, and modified
the steering as well as the longitudinal chassis members.
Qualifying, decided in those days by a lottery system – the
1933 Monaco Grand Prix was the first to rank the starters by
practice times – placed Nuvolari on the back row of the grid.
Ahead sat five Bugattis and five Alfa Romeos. By the end of the
first lap – 9.3 miles – Nuvolari had seized the lead and went
on to win the gruelling four-hour race by nearly four minutes.
This notable scalp, plus two other victories for Nuvolari that
season, bolstered Maserati's reputation at a crucial time for
the company.

Widened to meet the minimum-width regulations brought in with the 750kg formula, the 8CM-3000 remained competitive in lesser events into 1934 as Maserati prepared its new 3.7-litre inline-six engine, which promised to be 13kg lighter than the eight. But the new Grand Prix car, marketed as the 6C-34, arrived late in the year and was outgunned by competitors from Alfa Romeo, Mercedes and Auto Union. A development with a 4.2-litre V8, named the V8 RI – *Ruote Indipendenti*, signifying its independent suspension – won just one non-championship Grand Prix in which the German cars and Scuderia Ferrari were absent, though it found success in the USA (*see* Chapter 2).

The state-backed German cars brought new technologies and ideas (such as locating the engine behind the driver for better balance), lighter materials, sleeker aerodynamics, and horsepower-boosting fuel additives. Italy's competitors had no way of keeping up, not least the increasingly cash-poor Maserati. Nuvolari's fastest lap of Spa in an 8CM-3000 in 1933 had been 6m01s; four years later Hermann Lang went round in 5m04s in a Mercedes-Benz W125. Spooked by the sharp increase in speeds, the AIACR changed the rules again to cap engine sizes – but this did not change the picture of German domination. Once rescued by Adolfo Orsi, Maserati produced the 3-litre inline-eight 8CTF, which found success in the Indy 500 although unreliability blighted the car in Grands Prix – but in the absence of great European interest in its large-engined offerings, the company retreated to the 1.5-litre supercharged 'voiturette' class.

Maserati had been offering its 4CM ('Corsa Monoposto') model with both single-seat and sportscar bodies, and with supercharged inline-four engines from 1.1 litres to 2.5 litres, since 1931. Increased competition in the 'voiturette' class had rendered the 4CM obsolete, so in 1936 the brothers had

OVERLEAF: Franco Cortese battles with rivals in the 'voiturette' class aboard his 6CM in the 1937 German Grand Prix at the Nürburgring. Maserati did not have the resources to compete with Mercedes and Auto Union GP cars financed by the Nazi government.

BELOW: Almost 30 examples of the 6CM were built and it won the Targa Florio road race three times between 1937 and 1939.

unveiled the 6CM at the Milan Motor Show, based on the same chassis concept but with a supercharged 1.5-litre inline-six engine and independent front suspension. Production was stymied by the company's financial problems but, with Orsi's investment and the move to Modena, and impressive results on track, more customers began to beat a path to Maserati's door, including 1931 Le Mans 24 Hours winner and British Racing Drivers' Club co-founder Earl Howe. By the outbreak of war in 1939, 27 examples had been sold and Maserati's success in the class had even tempted Enzo Ferrari to follow suit: the Alfa Romeo 158, designed by Gioacchino Colombo, made its race debut in 1938. But while Maserati's successes in voiturette racing bolstered the brand's prestige, Alfa Romeo's apparent

capitulation in the top class caused political ructions and led to Ferrari's departure from the company's racing operations.

Despite developments to the engine which brought power from 155bhp to 175bhp, a lowering of the chassis rails, and aerodynamic fairings around the suspension, the relative competitiveness of the 6CM began to decline and Ernesto returned to the four-cylinder concept for its replacement. Introduced in 1939, the 4CL ('L' for 'linguette', meaning 'inline') was based on essentially the same chassis concept, but with a wider track and a lower stance. The new 1.5-litre engine featured an identical cylinder bore and stroke of 78cm, a higher compression ratio and a multi-valve head, blown by a more potent supercharger. All this, together with lower frictional

ABOVE: When racing began again after World War II it relied on pre-war cars and drivers to make up competitive grids. Here Louis Chiron, a month short of his 48th birthday, is pictured racing to second place in the 1947 Jersey Road Race aboard an eight-year-old 4CL.

ABOVE: Countess Howe, second wife of British Racing Drivers' Club president Earl Howe, presents a garland of flowers to Luigi Villoresi, winner of the 1948 British Grand Prix at Silverstone. Villoresi had started from the back of the field after the Maserati team was delayed in transit.

losses through having fewer moving parts, brought power to over 200bhp.

Initially, though, the new engine was unreliable. Humiliated on track by their German allies, the Italians in 1939 decided that all Grands Prix they organized would be for voiturettes only. On the 4CL's competitive debut, the Tripoli Grand Prix, Luigi Villoresi claimed pole position in one of three 4CLs entered – but all succumbed to engine issues as Hermann Lang and Rudolf Caracciola finished 1-2 in a pair of Mercedes W165 voiturettes which had been designed and built for this race in just eight months. The first race winner in a 4CL was a customer, the British privateer John Wakefield.

At the onset of World War II, Maserati spirited away 12 4CLs into the care of Arialdo Ruggeri, another amateur racer from a family made wealthy by its textile interests. Concealed

ABOVE: Seven Maseratis contested the 1950 Monaco Grand Prix, including this 4CLT/48 driven by Toulo de Graffenried.

in Milan, these cars would form the core of Maserati's racing activities when competition got underway again – remarkably quickly – after hostilities ceased. The first peacetime motor race, the Coupes de Paris, was held in the French capital on 9 September 1945. Scarcity of materials and the damaged economies of Europe dictated that motor racing was the preserve of those cars which had been successfully hidden from looters, conquerors, and those who would have melted them down for munitions and army vehicles. Ruggeri's Scuderia Milano team, founded in 1946, became a key ally to the factory in the post-war racing scene, even fielding a new 8CL for Luigi Villoresi and a 4CL for Duke Nalon in the Indy 500.

Equipped with a 4CL, Villoresi won what is believed to be the first post-war Grand Prix, on a street circuit in Nice in April 1946; across the Atlantic, the first post-war street race

BELOW: 4CLT chassis
1600, originally bought
by Argentina's national
car club with financial
support from President
Juan Péron and raced
by Juan Manuel Fangio,
still competes in historic
events today.

took place in the village of Watkins Glen in upstate New York in 1948. George Weaver led the first two laps in his recently acquired Maserati V8RI, nicknamed 'Poison Lil'. Between these historically significant events, a Maserati 8CTF won the Pikes Peak hillclimb twice in the hands of Louis Unser. 6CMs and 4CLs formed the bulk of the grids in many post-war races, which were mostly run to Formula Libre rules to attract as many entrants as possible. Later in the decade, racing's governing body essentially inked in the voiturette as the car of choice when it codified Formula A, later known as Formula 1, based around cars with up to 1.5-litre supercharged or up to 4.5-litre naturally aspirated engines. The intention was to build towards a world championship for drivers, beginning in 1950.

Alfa Romeo had also successfully concealed its 158s and

to contend with these Ernesto Maserati evaluated several modifications to the 4CL, chiefly to combat chassis flex. The fruit of this was the 4CLT, which featured tubular rather than box-section chassis rails, forged rather than cast suspension uprights, and a new crankshaft bearing design for the engine as well as twin superchargers. Alberto Ascari won on the car's first appearance, the 1948 San Remo Grand Prix, and it went on to win many more prestigious races including the two British Grands Prix held at Silverstone before that circuit hosted the inaugural world championship race in 1950.

By then the Maserati brothers had departed the company they founded, but there was sufficient strength in depth in the organization to keep the 4CLT competitively quick through engine developments and lightweighting. But it was not quite

ABOVE: In 1957 Maserati evaluated a V12 engine in the 250F.

OPPOSITE: Scarcity of Formula 1 cars meant the world championship races of 1952–53 were open to F2 cars only. The A6GCM, seen here at the 1952 French GP in the hands of Philippe Étancelin, only challenged the dominant Ferraris after engine and chassis revisions.

quick enough as Alfa Romeo unlocked more performance in the 158 through more aggressive supercharging and Enzo Ferrari reappeared under his own name with new V12-powered machinery. Louis Chiron's third place in the 1950 Monaco Grand Prix was as good as it got at world championship level.

Alberto Massimino and Ernesto Maserati had developed a sportscar racing cousin of the A6 road car, the A6GCS ('Corsa Sport'), which had proved successful enough for 15 examples to have been built and sold. In the post-brothers era Massimino worked with new recruit Vittorio Bellentani to develop the A6GCM single-seater for competition in the Formula 2 class, based on the standard ladder-frame chassis concept of the 4CLT and powered by a naturally aspirated two-litre DOHC inline-six engine producing 160bhp. The first two were sold straight into private hands in 1951. To produce more power Maserati revised the bore/stroke ratio of the engine in later cars,

unleashing a further 20bhp, but the greatest progress came with the arrival of Gioacchino Colombo in 1952. Following his input the engine's cylinder bore was increased and the stroke shortened, the cooling fins on the brake drums were enlarged, the rear suspension completely revised and the twin-spar chassis setup replaced by a stronger yet lighter network of triangulated tubes.

Not only did this transform the A6GCM into a race winner, it pointed the way to the company's next Formula 1 car. The world championship was adopting a 2.5-litre unsupercharged engine format for 1954 which would in theory offer competitors a clean slate with more modern cars. Enlarging the A6 engine architecture and carrying over the already proven chassis philosophy made the new project quick and straightforward. Maserati's offering would become one of the seminal Grand Prix cars of the 1950s.

The 250F was so closely based on the A6GCM that several examples of the F2 chassis had to be repurposed as F1 cars when demand outstripped supply at the beginning of 1954. It was known that Mercedes and Lancia were also working on bespoke cars for the new formula but these would not be ready until later in the year. Though Maserati had hoped for the 250F to be purely a customer car, the situation regarding supply required the factory to provide a great deal of operational support, albeit underwritten by outside finance.

Juan Manuel Fangio was contracted to Mercedes but, in order to score points, was 'loaned' to Maserati for the first two F1 Grands Prix of 1954 – which he won. Thereafter the 250F would claim just six more world championship wins but this was chiefly a factor of Mercedes' dominance for two seasons and Ferrari taking on the technically advanced D50 project for 1956 when Lancia, like Mercedes, withdrew from racing.

BELOW: Having won the first round of 1957 on home ground in Argentina, Fangio built towards a fourth consecutive world title with an imperious victory aboard his 250F in Monaco.

The 250F's historic significance goes beyond its modest record of victories. Perhaps most importantly, its presence in good numbers ensured healthy grids at a time when the world championship was on shaky ground, having had to adopt F2 cars from 1952–53 owing to the lack of competitive F1 entries. It was affordable and drivers loved its sweet handling balance. It offered great talents such as Stirling Moss a platform upon which to prove themselves. The first woman to race in F1, Maria Teresa de Filippis, did so in a 250F.

It was also the car in which Fangio clinched the last of his five world championships and his final Grand Prix win, one considered to be among the finest race drives of all time. When a long pitstop at the Nürburing in 1957 dropped him far away from the lead, Fangio broke the lap record of the 14-mile circuit nine times in 10 laps to catch and pass the Ferraris of Peter Collins and Mike Hawthorn.

The 250F's longevity is also a testament to the skill of Giulio Alfieri, who took over development after Colombo's departure and who designed a 2.5-litre V12 which was evaluated during 1957 before Maserati was forced to close its racing department. Ongoing financial difficulties militated against further involvement at the top level, although Alfieri designed a diminutive transverse-mounted V12 when F1 became a 1.5-litre naturally aspirated formula in 1961. While this never saw action, for the 'return to power' from 1966 onwards Alfieri cost-effectively enlarged the decade-old V12 design to three litres, powering John Surtees and Pedro Rodríguez to wins in Cooper cars.

OPPOSITE: Maria Teresa de Filippis was the first woman to race in Formula 1, starting three Grands Prix in 1958 in a 250F.

OVERLEAF: Fangio's victory in the 1957 German Grand Prix, where he broke the lap record nine times in ten laps while fighting back from a slow pitstop, is still considered one of the greatest drives of all time.

When Life Gives You Le Mans

Enter The Birdcage

Maserati's Grand Prix racing heritage in the pre-World War II era and post-war decade is such that it is easy to overlook the success the company enjoyed in sportscars and road racing at the time. Perhaps it is also because modern audiences view Formula 1 as the richest and most technologically advanced form of motorsport – whereas, up until the 1960s, sportscar racing was often more financially lucrative for drivers and manufacturers even if the cars were slightly less rarefied. It is also an unfortunate fact that, while Maserati has won Grands Prix and powered some of the most celebrated drivers of the 'golden era', success at the Le Mans 24 Hours has eluded the company.

When the French city of Le Mans hosted the first Grand Prix de l'ACF in 1906, the 24-hour endurance race which would become a celebrated annual event was 17 years away.
A month before the Grand Prix de l'ACF, Sicilian wine magnate Vincenzo Florio organized a race intended to be the sternest test of all: three laps of a 96-mile circuit around the Madonie mountains in northern Sicily, a perilous combination

OPPOSITE: The Tipo 61 cleverly subverted new windscreen height regulations.

of gradients, poor surfaces and free-roaming wildlife. The Targa Florio became infamous and would provide the stage for Maserati's first victory, Alfieri Maserati's class win in 1926 in a Tipo 26. The company also helped save the race when Alfa Romeo's dominance in the early 1930s chased away the majority of the other competitors and threatened to make the Targa Florio financially unviable. In 1937 the organizers were forced to relocate to the smaller 3.5-mile Parco della Favorita in Palermo and open the race to voiturettes; Francesco Severi won in a 6CM, kicking off four consecutive years of Maserati victories. Luigi Villoresi's win in May 1940 in a 4CL brought down the curtain on competitive motor racing in a Europe already embroiled in war.

The A6GCS provided Maserati with a presence in the world sportscar championship in the early 1950s, but it was not until Vittorio Bellentani reworked the engine and chassis of the 250F Grand Prix car into a two-seat sports-racer that the works team and its customers began to record significant results. American racer Bill Spear claimed a first podium for the 300S in the 1955 Sebring 12 Hours behind Mike Hawthorn in a Jaguar D-type and Phil Hill in a Ferrari 750 Monza, although the question of who actually finished first was not settled until a fortnight later owing to a protest by the Ferrari team. But while Maserati fielded a works team in 1956 with driving talent including Stirling Moss, Jean Behra and Carlos Menditiguy, and won 1000km races in Buenos Aires and at the Nürburging, it ultimately finished second in the championship to Ferrari. Furthermore, the Le Mans 24 Hours was off the calendar since its organizers had excluded sports-racers with engines larger than 2.5 litres in response to the catastrophic 1955 accident in which a driver and over 80 spectators had been killed.

For 1957 Maserati returned with Juan Manuel Fangio

now on the driver roster and a larger range of cars. As well as the 300S it had the 350S, with a strengthened chassis and a larger 3.5-litre straight six modified for competition from the 3500GT road car. Just three examples were built since this was viewed as a stopgap for the 450S, a big-engined sports-prototype the company had initially shelved after the 1955 Le Mans disaster. The impetus for rebooting this concept had come from a wealthy customer, US amateur

BELOW: One 450S was rebodied by Zagato in a coupé shell and raced at the 1957 Le Mans 24 Hours.

racer Tony Parravano, who had commissioned Maserati to build a 4.2-litre V8 for his Indycar. Expanding it to 4.5 litres and installing it in a modified 350S chassis revealed prodigious power – which would require much better braking and handling.

Fangio and Moss led the opening round of the 1957 season, the Buenos Aires 1000km, in the definitive 450S until its clutch failed. Fangio and Behra then won at Sebring but Maserati's championship was derailed by a series of different mechanical failures. At Le Mans – now back on the calendar after the organizers realigned themselves with the championship's rules – Maserati entered both a 'standard' 450S and one with a special streamlined bodyshell designed by Frank Costin, but both cars had retired by nightfall. Then, in the championship decider in Venezuela, catastrophe: Masten Gregory flipped the 450S entered by US racer Temple Buell on the second lap; Stirling Moss crashed into a wandering backmarker in one of the works 450Ss; and the other works 450S briefly caught fire in the pits before crashing out when the third factory Maserati, a 300S, suffered a tyre blow-out in front of it. The ruinous expense of the damage was a major contributor to Adolfo Orsi having to close the factory racing programme.

As Orsi tried to pry back control of the company from the administrators, in 1958 Alfieri drew up plans for a customer racing car using as much existing running gear as possible

BELOW: The company's financial difficulties prevented the 450S from fulfilling its potential, but its engine would enjoy a long life in Maserati's road car range.

and requiring few raw materials. Here the racing demands for light weight aligned perfectly with Maserati's tight budget. The new sports-racer, designated Tipo 60, was based on an extremely light structure of 200 small-gauge steel tubes welded together into a spaceframe. It was this which led to the Tipo 60 and its successors being nicknamed 'Birdcage'. With the 200bhp, 2-litre inline-four from the 200S installed the complete car weighed around 570kg, yielding a power-to-weight ratio of 350bhp per tonne. Canting the engine over at a 45-degree angle enabled it to be mounted lower, for better handling, and facilitated a distinctive and aerodynamically slippery body shape. The possibilities were extraordinary and Moss demonstrated the Tipo 60's potency by winning its first race, a sportscar event run on the Rouen Formula 2 Grand Prix weekend in August 1959.

In response to demand from US customers, Maserati subsequently produced the Tipo 61, powered by a 2.9-litre

version of the engine. 22 Tipo 60 and 61s were built, of which three went to American racer Lloyd 'Lucky' Casner's Camoradi team. Alfieri subsequently relocated the engine to behind the driver in the Tipo 63, 64 and 65 models, whose customers raced them in a variety of body shapes created by celebrated coachbuilders including Scaglione and Fantuzzi, and with V8 and V12 engines up to five litres.

But it is the Tipo 60 and 61s which are considered the seminal Maserati sports-racers of the 1960s even though, like the 250F single-seater, their roster of victories at the top level is less than extensive. Camoradi's Tipo 61s had the pace to win at Le Mans in 1960, Alfieri having interpreted new windscreen regulations more cleverly than Ferrari, but electrical issues cost them – Masten Gregory had a four-minute lead after a mighty opening stint, only for his car to be stuck in the pits for over an hour when it failed to restart. Another US customer, Briggs Cunningham, entered a Tipo

LEFT: The Tipo 60 (pictured) and larger-engined 61 models were based on the spaceframe-chassis concept of the 250F model, a network of around 200 small-diameter tubes – hence the 'Birdcage' nickname.

60 for himself and a pair of Tipo 63s the following year but once again time lost in the pits proved costly, and the highest-placed Maserati was a Tipo 63 co-driven by brewery heir Augie Pabst in fourth, behind three Ferraris.

As sportscar racing plunged into an expensive arms race during the 1960s, Maserati embarked on a toe-in-the-water exercise in the new closed-top category largely dominated by Ferrari's 250 GTO. Since the larger engines in latter Birdcages had challenged the ability of the small-gauge spaceframe to put down all that power, Alfieri returned to the traditional spaceframe concept for the Tipo 151, which located the four-litre quad-cam V8 ahead of the driver in a striking Kamm-tailed coupé bodyshell. Again the lack of development budget showed as the three cars failed to make the finish at Le Mans in 1962. Returning in 1963 with a five-litre engine installed in the Tipo 151, French racer André Simon had a mishap at the start when the hot sun made his door stick shut. Not only did he lose ground on his rivals, but in finally wrenching the door open, he struck himself in the face. Still bleeding from the nose, Simon seized the lead on the opening lap, only for the car to stick in gear later on with Casner at the wheel. The same chassis competed at Le Mans in 1964 and '65 in a new 'streamliner' bodyshell created by Carrozzeria Drogo, clocking a then-record top speed of 192mph. But the impetus for the project fizzled out when Casner flipped, with fatal consequences, during testing for the 1965 race.

Le Mans, then, remains unfinished business for the trident marque.

OPPOSITE: Just one of the three original Tipo 151s survives and fetched nearly £2m when last auctioned in 2006. At least one 'recreation' has been built.

OVERLEAF: All three Tipo 151s were entered for the 1962 Le Mans 24 Hours. Number 2, driven by Bruce McLaren and Walt Hansgen, lasted the longest, succumbing to diff failure in the 13th hour while running in fifth place.

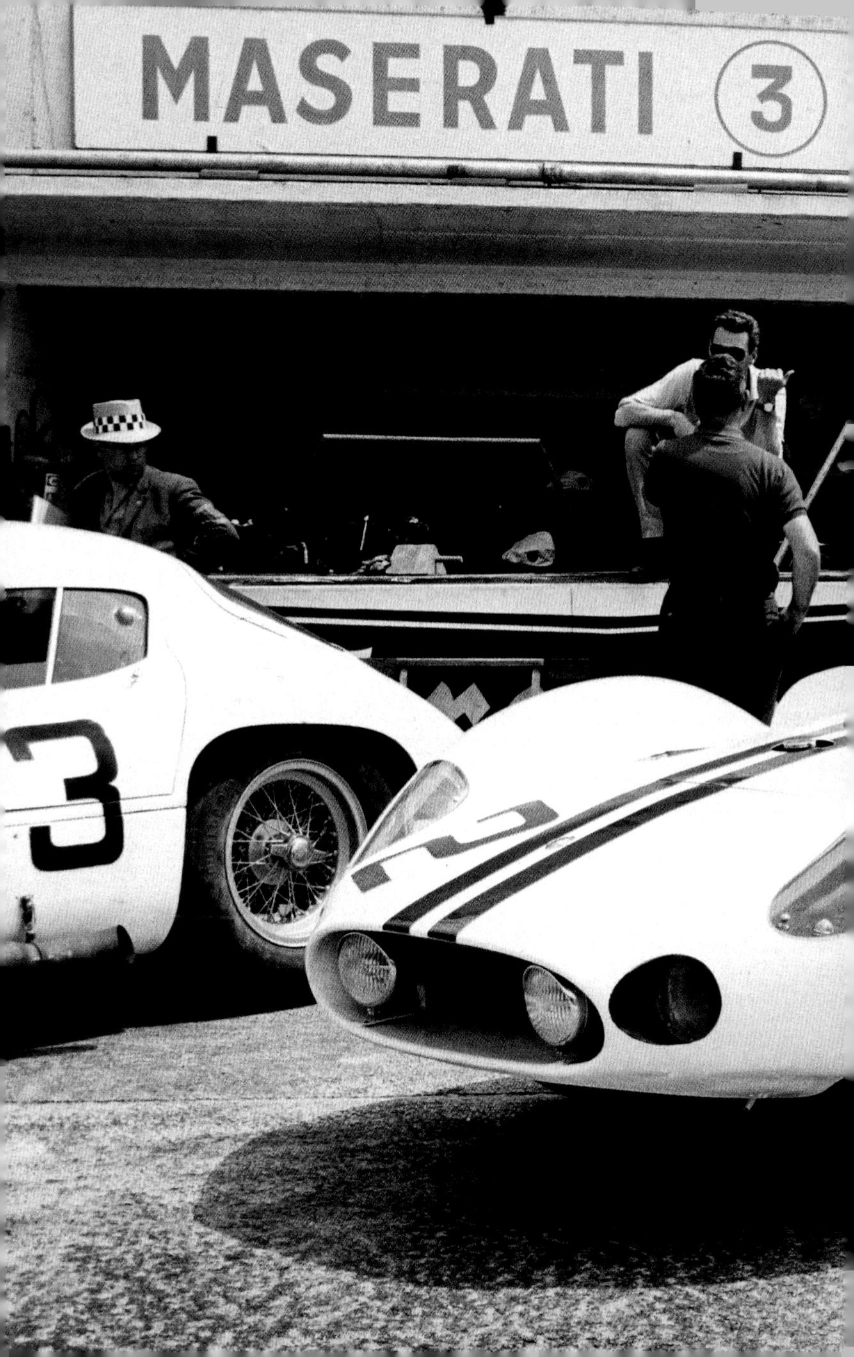
MASERATI 3

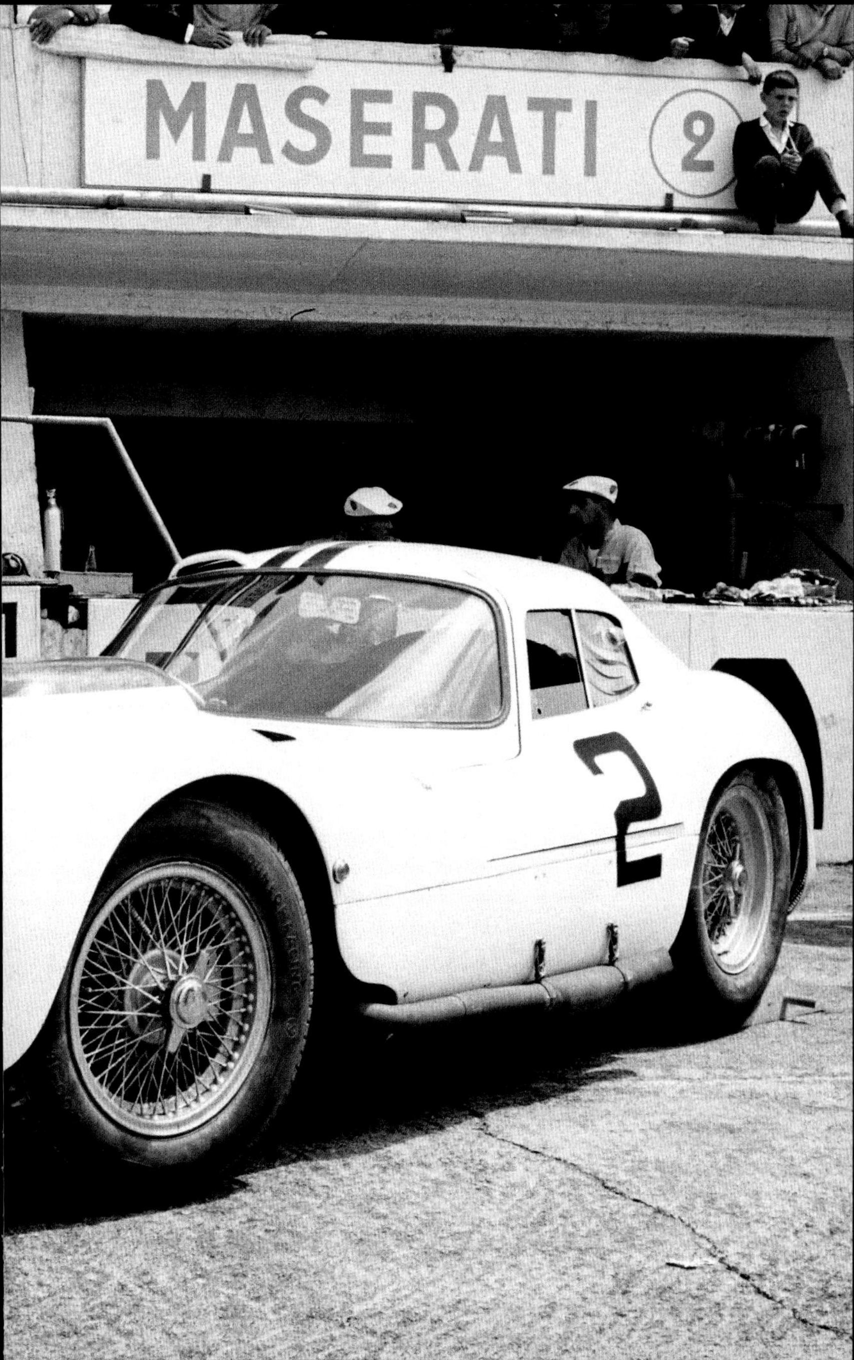
MASERATI 2
2

The French Correction

A Convenient Marriage

In 1969 Maserati's near-neighbour, Ferrari, became part of the Fiat empire in a deal which left Enzo Ferrari in control of his beloved racing activities but ultimately answerable to Fiat's suits in all other aspects of the business. It was an acknowledgement that the realities of car manufacture, even at the high end, were shifting towards mass production: faster, more consistent, and rigorously cost-controlled. The curtain was coming down on the era of hand-built sportscars of which no two examples were quite the same. Businesses that specialized in the bespoke were going to have to learn to stamp their basic products out of a mould.

Maserati had already begun its journey down that road but with a somewhat more unusual companion. The French car manufacturer Citroën had acquired a reputation for innovative engineering through its mould-breaking Traction Avant, the first mass-produced front-wheel-drive car, the 2CV – among the definitive post-war economy vehicles – and the DS, a sleek saloon which rode on sophisticated hydropneumatic suspension. Launched in 1955, the DS still looked futuristic

OPPOSITE: Citroën's SM featured a Maserati-built V6 engine.

BELOW: Giulio Alfieri
– pictured here with
Stirling Moss at the
1954 Italian Grand Prix –
remained a key figure in
Maserati's car and engine
development through
the Citroën era.

a decade later. And Citroën's intention was to capitalize on the bold spirit of the 1960s by offering a performance variant of it: the inline-four engine under the bonnet of the DS could trace its ancestry back to the 1930s, a putative flat-six engine having been abandoned late in the day.

Under the codename 'Project S' the company had been evaluating a series of prototypes since the beginning of the decade but had yet to alight on a suitable engine concept. Walter Becchia, designer of the 2CV's flat-twin, was working on a six-cylinder engine while Citroën also formed what would be an abortive partnership with German manufacturer NSU to create a triple-rotor Wankel rotary unit. Amid uncertainty over the production viability of these engines, in January 1968 Citroën approached Maserati to design and build a 2.7-litre V6. By the end of the year these negotiations had bloomed

into a full-scale acquisition in which Citroën bought 60 per cent of Maserati, leaving Adolfo Orsi with 40 per cent and a position as honorary chairman. Omar Orsi stayed on the board of directors.

Giulio Alfieri was given six months to design the new engine but accomplished it in three weeks. The initial brief was for the new V6 to be light and compact, no larger physically than the existing inline-four, and (to accommodate French taxation boundaries) displacing no more than 2.7 litres. Alfieri based the prototype on the 4.2-litre version of his classic V8 he had developed for the new Maserati Indy road car, which was replacing the ageing Quattroporte and Sebring models. Removing two cylinders, narrowing the bore slightly and reducing the stroke yielded a 2.7-litre V6 capable of far more than the 150bhp laid down in the brief, though the final production unit shared only its 90-degree cylinder angle and

ABOVE: The SM's mechanical complexity – note the green pressurized spheres for the hydropneumatic suspension crowding the engine – put off many potential owners.

BELOW: With a drag
coefficient of 0.34
the Citroën's sleek,
futuristic bodyshell
was remarkably
aerodynamic.

the cam followers with the prototype. The definitive engine
layout was expandable (through a longer stroke) to three litres
for overseas markets, primarily the US, and it would also later
be downsized to two when the Italian government brought in
a new tax regime punishing larger-engined cars. Fitting the
five-speed Citroën gearbox at the front enabled the engine to be
mounted behind the front wheels, improving car balance.

Two design decisions would prove problematic, though.
V6s have a less even firing order than V8s and generally have a
narrower included angle to mitigate the vibrations that result.
Retaining the 90-degree angle required counterweights on the
crankshaft which added inertia, dampening throttle response.
More critically the primary tensioners for the chains driving

the four overhead camshafts would prove insufficiently durable despite extensive testing. Maserati historians generally place the blame for this on Citroën engineers disregarding advice to use a stronger component on the grounds that these had seen service in the DS since the 1950s without issue.

Project S became one of the most significant new launches at the 1970 Geneva Motor Show. While the suspension was an uprated version of the system used on the DS – which remained years ahead of the steel springs and oil dampers employed by other car manufacturers – every other aspect of the SM was a step up which befitted its more elevated position in the model range. Brakes were now discs all round and the self-centring, speed-sensitive power steering was a fast two

turns from lock to lock. It also swivelled two of the six Cibie halogen headlights mounted in the fully glazed nose. Robert Opron's sleek bodyshell, tapering behind a long nose to flush rear wheels, had a remarkably low drag coefficient of 0.34 and remains starkly modern to this day, over five decades later. Not only did the SM offer a driving experience like no other, with its supple ride, rapid steering and brakes, and offbeat V6 growl, it inked in Citroën's status as a visionary car maker.

While the work of historian Marc Sonnery has done much to correct the long-held belief among Maserati purists that Citroën micromanaged its Italian outpost to the company's detriment, the response to early failures of the V6 demonstrates the flaws of Citroën's more bureaucratic approach. As customers returned SMs whose valves had enjoyed rather too close society with the pistons after the chain tensioners failed, the diktat came down from Paris to mend or replace broken engines rather than adopt a stronger component on the production line. As a result the SM acquired a reputation for unreliability and sales plummeted after strong early interest.

By 1971 the Orsis had come to the realization that their role was essentially ceremonial and Adolfo sold his 40 per cent stake to Citroën. Under French ownership Maserati was busily using the fresh investment to revise a model range which had begun to grow long in the tooth. The Mexico, named to commemorate John Surtees' 1966 Mexican Grand Prix victory in a Maserati-engined Cooper F1 car, found favour with celebrities including actor-turned-politician Ronald Reagan but was rather staid to drive; and the Ghibli, despite the attractions of its svelte styling (the early work of celebrated designer Giorgetto Giugiaro), suffered from a primitive rigid-propshaft arrangement which transmitted much drivetrain harshness through the suspension and into the body. Performance was never lacking but the perception of outdatedness was leading

Maserati to be viewed as a poor man's Ferrari, if such a thing
could actually exist.

Named – like the Ghibli – after a wind, the Bora, launched
at the 1971 Geneva Motor Show, was a timely course correction
and the first new Maserati developed under Citroën's
custodianship. Guy Mallaret, installed as Maserati's general
manager by Citroën, had an eye on broader developments in
the racing scene and in 1969 pitched Giulio Alfieri the idea
of a two seater-mid-engined sportscar. At Le Mans Ford's
mid-engined GT40 had humbled Ferrari, and Lamborghini's
Miura, powered by a V12 mounted transversely behind the
cockpit, was the most exciting and quick road car of the

BELOW: Low-slung seats and a dashboard with instruments built into the centre of a spokeless steering wheel completed the futuristic feel of the Boomerang concept.

era. Enzo Ferrari, though, was so averse to the engine being anywhere but ahead of the driver that his company's 1967 mid-engined coupé had been marketed under the Dino sub-brand, without a Ferrari logo on it.

Alfieri needed no further prompting. Having been stymied by lack of development funds for the Tipo 63, 64 and 65 racing cars, he was determined to make use of the opportunity.

Giugiaro was engaged to design a bodyshell, which bore a familial resemblance to the Ghibli, while work proceeded on a unitary bodyshell which would feature fully independent suspension for the first time in a Maserati road car. The final shape shared a number of features with the Ghibli, including the nose and pop-up headlamps, but naturally differed in stance and proportions owing to the engine's new location.

Brushed stainless steel on the window trims and A-pillars contrasted with the painted bodyshell and black belt line in a tasteful embrace of the wedge shape which was becoming fashionable at the time.

Development was marred by clashes between Alfieri and Guerrino Bertocchi, the engineer who also acted as Maserati's chief test driver. Though gifted behind the wheel – he was fond of telling interviewers he had been as fast as Maserati's Grand Prix drivers – Bertocchi was set in his ways, having been at the company since 1926. He disliked the notion of a mid-engined, GT car, fought against it, and was happy to share his opinions with anyone prepared to listen – indeed, he was eventually fired after being caught advising customers to buy De Tomaso's Pantera instead.

Although the longitudinally mounted 4.7-litre V8 was carried over from the Ghibli, the five-speed gearbox was bought in from ZF, while the braking system came from the Citroën parts catalogue. The engine and gearbox were located within a separate subframe mounted to the body via rubber bushes to reduce noise and vibrations; an access panel at the back of the cockpit was concealed under thick carpet to reduce the impact

ABOVE: As evidence of Maserati's creative energy, and new investment under Citroën ownership, the Giugiaro-designed Boomerang showcar wowed visitors to the 1972 Geneva Show just months after the launch of the mid-engined Bora.

ABOVE: The Bora had a familial resemblance to the Ghibli in its details but the shorter bonnet gave away the fact that the engine was mounted behind the passenger compartment.

of drivetrain din on the occupants. Later Maserati would add a 4.9-litre engine option, primarily for the US market.

Given the conceptual differences between the Ghibli and Bora, the newer car was offered alongside the existing model rather than replacing it. But sales of both – and the Citroën SM – were hit by the spike in oil prices in 1973 following the outbreak of hostilities in the Middle East. When oil-producing nations placed an embargo on countries which had supported Israel during the Yom Kippur war, the sudden contraction in supply sent further shocks through economies already affected by weakening stock markets.

Maserati had only just introduced another post-Citroën model, the Merak, also styled by Giugiaro but with a smaller engine – a three-litre version of the SM's V6 – enabling the cockpit to accommodate two smaller 'occasional' seats behind

the driver and passenger. Although the Merak was named after
a star in the constellation of Ursa Minor, rather than a wind,
it was identical to the Bora from nose to doors. As well as the
braking system many interior elements, including the entire
instrument panel, came from Citroën.

ABOVE: Citroën's
influence was clear
to see in the Merak's
interior, where the
steering wheel and
instrument panel were
identical to the SM's.

The timing of the oil crisis coincided inauspiciously with
the launch of another new Maserati at the 1973 Paris Salon,
a conceptual replacement for the Ghibli, also named after a
desert wind: the Khamsin. Designed by Marcello Gandini
at Bertone, the Khamsin is now regarded as something of a
forgotten gem in the designer's canon – perhaps because his
seminal Lamborghini Countach, a product of the same era, has
taken all the oxygen. It is somewhat conservative in comparison
but that is because the Khamsin was conceived as an elegant
and subtle grand tourer rather than an eye-catching supercar.

In five-litre form the V8 delivered plenty of acceleration with a suitably effortless torque curve, despite a proliferation of Citroën-derived hydraulic systems drawing power for the brakes and steering.

Maserati was also working on a successor to the Quattroporte and had got as far as building a prototype – Gandini styling on top of a Citroën SM floorpan, with a new front-mounted four-litre V8 engine based on the architecture of the SM's V6 – when the walls caved in. Citroën was facing a financial crisis of its own and could no longer afford to sustain an Italian subsidiary building cars for a denuded market. In June 1974 Michelin, Citroën's parent company, announced a 'merger' with French rival Peugeot; in fact it was more akin to a sale. Within months Peugeot's accountants were

drawing red lines through various expensive projects including the SM, which was duly axed and many spare parts destroyed, and Maserati, which was put into liquidation in May 1975.

Alejandro de Tomaso, who had tried to acquire Maserati the previous decade, would get his prize after all. With financial support from the Italian government – which could ill-afford so many employers going bust – De Tomaso had been picking up distressed assets all over the country, including the coachbuilders Vignale and Ghia, and motorcycle manufacturers Moto Guzzi and Benelli. In August 1975 he added Maserati to his portfolio.

It is said that Giulio Alfieri played a key role in steering Adolfo Orsi towards Citroën rather than De Tomaso in 1968, and that this was the motivation for what happened next. Shortly after the takeover he arrived for work to find the contents of his office in the car park. His replacement was Aurelio Bertocchi, the son of his old sparring partner Guerrino...

ABOVE: Styled by Giugiaro, the Medici II pointed the way to the definitive Series III Quattroporte. The working prototype was sold to the Shah of Persia.

Changing Hands

A Decade of Decline

Alejandro de Tomaso remains a polarizing figure for Maserati aficionados. Neverthless his intervention came at a time when Peugeot–Citroën had made the workforce redundant, and the workers had responded by blockading the factory: not an epoch in which any cars were likely to be built.

De Tomaso's modus operandi while snapping up distressed Italian businesses in the mid-1970s was to reduce the financial risk to himself by maintaining a minority shareholding via a holding company, while the majority of shares were owned by *Società per le Gestioni e Partecipazioni Industriali* (GEPI), a state-owned entity. Nevertheless he was granted full control of the businesses despite the lop-sided ownership structure; as a one-time racing driver and owner of his own eponymous marque, he was better placed to direct Maserati than some faceless technocrat with no interest in or knowledge of cars.

The new proprietor had the right instincts in terms of Maserati's direction but the execution was wanting. Ruthlessness was a De Tomaso trademark: this was a man who had left a failed political career in his native Argentina at the

OPPOSITE: Alejandro de Tomaso had tried to buy Maserati in the late 1960s.

OPPOSITE: In the
recession of the late
1970s and early 1980s,
Maserati marketing
focused on low pricing.

age of 26, also abandoning his wife and children in the process, to set himself up as a racing driver and entrepreneur in Italy, where he had remarried into money. Apart from culling half of the workforce, his early moves included a purge of all Citroën-derived components in the model range simply because he didn't like the marque. While most of this would have escaped the notice of owners, it did extend to a complete revamp of the Merak's interior to something more in keeping with the brand.

De Tomaso also wanted to underline the fact this was the start of a new era by launching a new model. Given the scarcity of resources, including time, ahead of the 1976 show season, the 'new' car would actually be a reskinned version of a De Tomaso car which had already been in production for four years. Based around a somewhat primitive ladder chassis (albeit one designed by Gianpaolo Dallara, one of the 'fathers' of the Lamborghini Miura) and a Ford-sourced V8 engine, the Longchamp had been styled by Ghia's Tom Tjaarda, designer of the Ferrari 330 GT2+2 and 365 California. It wore its Ford sources in plain sight, including the headlamps, which were sourced from the Granada saloon. In executing a mild nose-and-tail job to transform the donor vehicle into the Maserati Kyalami – named after the circuit where Pedro Rodríguez won the 1967 South African Grand Prix in a Cooper Maserati – veteran stylist and coachbuilder Pietro Frua dispensed with these incongruous relics from the Ford parts bin. Frua had also designed the original Maserati Quattroporte and Mistral.

Naturally the Longchamp's Ford engine made way for a Maserati V8 – a 4.2-litre version of the extant eight-cylinder rather than the new one developed for the Quattroporte II, which De Tomaso axed. The car was not a massive sales success, reaching 200 customers in seven years of production – but neither was the Longchamp a hit, selling 410 in its 17-year life. Still, these figures dwarf those of the car that is perhaps

We've put the cat amongst the pigeons.

Now you can own one of the world's classic cars for less than you think.

Less, in fact, than most of the other exhilarating modes of transport you may be considering.

Ferrari 308 GTB	£20,100
Mercedes 380 SLC	£21,530
Porsche 928	£21,827
Maserati Merak	£18,987

And Maserati prices are down across the whole magnificent range.

A range of motor cars that is still very much in a class of its own.

Breathtaking performance.

The race bred handling. And the unsurpassed luxury and refinement. That's the beauty of owning and driving one of the world's great cars.

Cars like the exquisite mid-engined Merak SS. The executive 5-seater Kyalami with engine and transmission options. And the ultimate in high performance cars — the incredible 169 mph Khamsin powered by a 4.9 litre V8 with manual gearbox.

Maserati prices start at only £18,987 including air conditioning.

Talk Maserati. And watch the feathers fly. ⓜ *Maserati*

BELOW: In 1977 the
Khamsin was facelifted,
gaining three slots in
the nose and losing a lot
of the Citroën-derived
components.

the most niche production Maserati of all: built to order for
territories which did not require European Type Approval, the
Quattroporte II – powered by the three-litre ex-SM V6 – found
12 customers between 1976 and '78.

Fuel prices continued to be an issue for the performance car
market, as did – albeit more locally – the Italian government's
fiscal manoeuvrings. In 1977 the IVA purchase tax was
doubled to 38 per cent for cars with engines displacing over
two litres. Maserati, like Ferrari, responded by introducing
variants specifically for the Italian market. The two-litre Merak
could reach nearly 140mph given a flat and long enough stretch
of road.

Another pillar of De Tomaso's new-model strategy would
be a successor to that perennial 1960s favourite of the rich and
famous, the Quattroporte. The original had sold in respectable
numbers to a rarefied clientele. In the interregnum between the

end of production in 1969 and the attempt to develop a front-wheel-drive model under Citroën's ownership, Pietro Frua had designed and built two examples based on the Maserati Indy chassis; one was commissioned by the Aga Khan, the other was said to have gone to the King of Spain. While the definitive third-generation Quattroporte was shown in prototype form at the Turin Motor Show in 1976, part of De Tomaso's rush to put new models on display, it did not reach production until 1979.

The Quattroporte III's chassis was essentially another hand-me-down from De Tomaso, originally designed for the Deauville before being shortened for the Longchamp and Maserati Kyalami. If the Giugiaro-styled body also seemed vaguely familiar, that's because his ItalDesign company had already built Maserati Indy-based show cars badged as the Medici I and II as design studies for a putative four-door

BELOW: The more powerful Merak SS model arrived in 1975, later joined by a two-litre model aimed at the Italian market.

ABOVE: Opulence and conservativism defined the interior of the third-gen Quattroporte.

hatchback. For the third-generation Quattroporte Giugiaro repurposed a number of design features, particularly at the front end, to produce a sober but purposeful and elegant four-door saloon bodyshell with four square headlamps flanking the trident logo up front. The interior also featured the bar and fridge which were signature touches of the Medici II, later sold to the Shah of Persia shortly before his deposition in the Iranian revolution. At four metres long and weighing two tonnes, this was a car in which one made stately progress regardless of whether the 4.2 or 4.9-litre V8 had been specified. It was a favourite of Italian President Alessandro Pertini and opera singer Luciano Pavarotti, whose enthusiastic patronage led to over 2,100 examples being sold.

If the natural buyers of the Quattroporte were royalty, the political elite and celebrities – and therefore largely recession-proof – Maserati also needed a means of tapping into a broader market which was still affected by the decade's economic shocks. It was becoming increasingly difficult to get into the US, owing to emissions regulations and the imposition of disfiguring crash-protection measures such as large rubber bumpers. De Tomaso believed the answer lay in a car which could be produced in large volumes and considerably undercut opposition from the likes of Porsche and Ferrari on price.

Stylistically the 1981 Biturbo owed a debt to BMW's front-engine, rear-drive 3-Series. Designed in-house by Pierangelo Andreani, it straddled the worlds of the sports saloon and coupé: a two-door saloon bodyshell with a well-proportioned glasshouse and features derived from existing models in the lineup, particularly the nose and tail of the Quattroporte. It was a very different beast from the Khamsin and the Bora, which were being quietly dropped from the range. If its sobriety seems peculiar to modern eyes, it was entirely in keeping with an era of social unrest in which ostentatious displays of wealth were off the menu for buyers who did not travel with a security detail. Using the two-litre version of the V6 enabled Maserati to circumvent Italy's punitive IVA; a pair of small IHI turbochargers, one for each cylinder bank, brought power to 180bhp without incurring the 'lag' in delivery suffered by larger turbo impellers.

Maserati's official history includes the caveat "first-generation versions challenged the factory's production capacity". This is the company being considerably economical with the *actualité*, although the Biturbo does not really deserve its place in the countless lazily written 'listicles' of the world's worst cars which populate the internet. Certainly the rapid scaling-up of production to meet the enthusiastic initial

BELOW: Just over 1800
Meraks were built
between 1972 and 1983
– modest numbers but
more than double those
of the rival Lamborghini
Urraco.

demand – using the Innocenti car factory to manufacture
various elements – brought quality-control problems, but the
rushed development phase also baked in certain undesirable
characteristics. Figures within Maserati at the time blame
De Tomaso for targeting an unrealistically low price point,
such that corners had to be cut – there was no budget for a
cover for the spare wheel which hung below the boot, where it
was a permanent eyesore.

Cheap materials meant the interior palpably looked built
down to a price when new, and wore poorly. Inferior-quality
steel – in fairness, an inherent problem for the Italian car

industry at the time – led to issues with rust. The engines were prone to overheating which required expensive rebuilds, and the electrics needed little prompting to go into meltdown. Reputational damage dented sales but Maserati continued to develop the Biturbo, adding the S model in 1983 with a much needed intercooler along with a higher compression ratio, bringing power to 205bhp. A 2.5-litre model was added for the export market in the same year.

De Tomaso was determined to milk the Biturbo format for all it was worth. Through the 1980s new variants appeared almost by the week, including the Biturbo 425, a four-door

version with a wheelbase extended by 86mm. Alongside this Maserati introduced a new model to replace the moribund Kyalami: wider, longer and taller than the Biturbo and based on a lengthened version of that car's chassis, the two-door 228 model aimed to bridge the gap in the range between the Biturbo and the Quattroporte. Mechanically similar to the Biturbo as well as bearing a strong family resemblance – they were chiefly distinguishable by the bigger car having a broader-rimmed chrome grille – the 228 had a larger 2.8-litre version of the twin-turbo V6 producing 250bhp, enough to propel the car from 0–60mph in six seconds. The interior was also more opulently trimmed, as befitted a more premium price point. But by the time the 228 reached the market in 1986, the Biturbo's early quality issues had tarnished Maserati's reputation to the point that it barely registered a blip in the sales charts – particularly in the US market at which it was so clearly aimed.

Still, the company had done enough to attract the interest of Lee Iacocca, head of US giant Chrysler and self-defined 'car guy'. In the 1980s he was on an acquisition trail that would lead to Lamborghini entering US ownership, but his company's relationship with Maserati would be a fleeting one – thankfully. Iacocca believed it was possible and indeed desirable to spread premium glitter on humdrum machinery by adding a well-known badge. The result was the Chrysler TC by Maserati, a badge-engineered horror based on a shortened version of the K platform which had spawned the Chrysler LeBaron and Dodge Daytona. Initially powered by the Daytona's 2.2-litre turbocharged inline-four, driving through a three-speed automatic gearbox, it lumbered from 0-60mph in an unimpressive 11 seconds. The model lasted three years from launch in 1986, cycling through three different engine variants (latterly a Mistubishi V6) to diminishing interest. Little wonder, since it cost twice as much as a LeBaron and had little to show for it except for the Maserati trident within the Chrysler logo on the nose.

Maserati kept the Biturbo alive through a Zagato-engineered convertible variant in 1984, followed by a Marcello Gandini restyle of the tin-top model in 1987 and the introduction of the Kharif coupé in 1988. Dropping the Biturbo name in favour of number-based nomenclature put some distance between the

BELOW: Zagato designed and engineered a convertible version of the Biturbo in 1984.

326 Horses.

Almost an unfair advantage.

OPPOSITE: The Shamal
two-door coupé carried
over a great deal of
the Biturbo, including
the doors – and the
architecture of the new
V8 engine was based on
the Biturbo's V6, too.

car and its troubled early years, but not enough for Maserati to escape niche manufacturer status: when the Gandini-designed, twin-turbo V8 Shamal was launched in 1989, among the more obvious evidence of Maserati's tight financial circumstances were the carry-over doors and interior from the Biturbo. Such budget as existed had been spent on developing the all-new engine, a definitive break from a family line which had begun with the 450S in 1956.

Faced with continued operating losses, De Tomaso had to seek outside investment to buy out GEPI's interest in the company. In 1990 Fiat took a 49 per cent shareholding in Maserati; Innocenti was split off from the company and its factory in Lambrate closed two years later.

After another Gandini restyle in 1990, the Biturbo gave way to the Ghibli II in 1992. Development budgets dictated little change to the bodyshell and interior, though the engine range received a mild performance uplift. There were plans to introduce a mid-engined sportscar to be called the Chubasco but it was deemed too expensive to build so the concept was recycled into the Barchetta, a two-seater racing car with a backbone chassis based on the De Tomaso Guara; with this Maserati aimed to stage a potentially lucrative one-make racing series for high-net-worth customers.

This idea fell by the wayside after Alejandro de Tomaso suffered a stroke in 1993. Although he subsequently recovered, declining health prompted him to remove himself from public life, place his son in charge of his eponymous car company, and sell the remainder of his shares in Maserati to Gianni Agnelli's Fiat empire. Rivals for so long, Maserati and Ferrari would now have to find a way to coexist.

Joining the
Neighbours

The Trident and the Prancing Horse

For the best part of four years Maserati existed in a sort of limbo, the proverbial elephant in the room for an industrial empire which also included Ferrari, at one time Maserati's bitter rival on track. Such were the entrenched cultural divisions between the two marques that aficionados of each – particularly in the Modena area – preferred not to speak the name of the other.

As the cliché goes, the squeakiest hinges get the most oil. And in the early 1990s Ferrari, for so long the Fiat group's halo brand, was almost permanently in crisis. Infighting after Enzo Ferrari's death in 1988 had rendered the Formula 1 team almost a national embarrassment – it went winless for three seasons between 1991 and '93 – and the 348, its 'volume' road model, was well outclassed by rivals. Fiat's suits patently failed to understand the performance car business and it was not until Fiat magnate Gianni Agnelli drafted in Luca di Montezemolo, Ferrari's F1 team manager in the glory days of the mid-1970s and more recently an architect of the successful Italia '90 football World Cup, that the company entered turnaround.

OPPOSITE: New ownership restored the value of the brand.

Amid the corporate firefighting up the road at Maranello, Maserati quietly got on with a policy of 'more of the same' in product terms. At the 1994 Geneva Motor Show the company unveiled a mildly restyled Ghibli II with a refreshed interior, larger wheels, electronically adjustable suspension and anti-lock brakes, the latter elements simply keeping up with modern performance car trends. A month later, in Turin, Maserati revealed its first post-De Tomaso product: the fourth-generation Quattroporte, based on a stretched version of the Biturbo chassis and powered by the twin-turbo V6 2.8-litre V6 as used in the Ghibli II (the two-litre was also offered for the Italian market). Again, Marcello Gandini was responsible for

the exterior, essentially a modernized take on what had gone before; the most obvious points of difference were the interior, which was more richly trimmed, and the driving experience, which was more sprightly since the car was up to 300kg lighter depending on engine choice. Eighteen months later another variant joined the range, featuring the new all-aluminium V8 as used in the Shamal.

Otherwise, Maserati existed in a quiet backwater of the Fiat empire – until a major scandal erupted in 1996. As part of the official transfer of assets between entities old and new during Fiat's acquisition, Alejandro de Tomaso had in effect retained ownership of 19 historic Maseratis on display in the company

museum. Besides examples of the first-generation Quattroporte it included race cars with cherished history, including a V12-engined 250F, the Drogo-bodied Tipo 61 'Birdcage' in which Masten Gregory and Lloyd Casner won the 1961 Nürburgring 1000kms, and the one-off 420M/58 raced by Stirling Moss in the 1958 'Monzanapolis' Race of Two Worlds with sponsorship from the Eldorado ice cream company – one of the earliest examples of on-car sponsor branding in European motor racing. In July 1996 De Tomaso had the cars removed and sent to England, where they were subsequently advertised for sale by auction.

This news caused sensation and outrage in Modena. But the cars had already gone – it was claimed by some sources that they had been offered to Fiat, but the company was not interested in buying. Local anger reached the seat of national government; even the minister for culture got involved. But there would be no rescue from the taxpayer this time. Private capital was required – and it arrived in the form of Umberto Panini, brother of football trading card magnate Giuseppe Panini. The auction house removed the cars from sale and they were returned to Italy, where Umberto accommodated them in a new museum on his farm.

Fiat may or may not have been offered the historic machinery but it now identified Maserati as a problem which needed to be solved. Under Montezemolo, Ferrari's F1 team was returning to competitiveness and its road car range was improving in performance, modernity and quality. It seemed logical to Agnelli to expand Montezemolo's remit to incorporate Maserati – and, courtesy of some financial engineering within the Fiat Group, Maserati became a 50 per cent subsidiary of Ferrari in 1997. Montezemolo would later describe the scene when he first visited the Maserati works at the Viale Ciro Menotti as "a peaceful home for stray cats".

OPPOSITE: Having turned Ferrari around in the early 1990s, Luca di Montezemolo mapped out a similar plan for Maserati.

ABOVE: Maserati's first all-new model under Fiat ownership, the 3200 GT was a vital step in the company's evolution.

A clean break was required, both in terms of the model range and the means of production. As Ferrari drew up plans for a new facility to replace the existing factory in Modena (ultimately only some external walls would remain), it pushed through development of a new model to replace the Shamal and begin the process of repositioning Maserati as a slightly softer and more luxurious brand. Initially the intention was to continue the tradition of naming Maseratis after winds, but the chosen name – Mistral – had already been registered by the Volkswagen Group, so instead the company looked further back in history to its first production grand tourer, the 3500 GT. Since the new car was to be powered by an evolution of the Shamal's twin-turbo 3.2-litre V8, it was named the 3200 GT.

Giorgetto Giugiaro was responsible for styling the bodyshell, neatly accomplishing the feat of incorporating some recognizable flourishes from previous Maseratis without veering into pastiche. And Giugiaro himself was present, alongside Stirling Moss, when Montezemolo presented the 3200 GT to the world's press in September 1998, just before the Paris Motor Show. By then Maserati was in dire need of the car. Despite the unveiling earlier that year of the Quattroporte Evoluzione, a refreshed model claiming to have 50 per cent new parts, Maserati managed to sell a little over 500 cars worldwide in 1998.

From this nadir the recovery was rapid. In 2000, as the new buildings on Viale Ciro Menotti approached completion, Maserati moved four times as many units as it had two years earlier. The 3200 GT proved transformative, even though

BELOW: The Spyder
signalled Maserati's
imminent re-entry
into the important
US market.

when pushed to the limits of adhesion it began to show some of the truculent manners of the company's previous proprietor. These traits were accentuated slightly in the automatic model, introduced in 1999: circumstances dictated that the four-speed gearbox was bought in rather than developed in-house, and it occasionally struggled to transmit the V8's prodigious torque to the road in a decorous fashion. Not that this dissuaded buyers, and the 3200 GT's success moved Montezemolo to persuade Fiat to grant Ferrari 100 per cent control of the company.

Maserati's future was now clear: along with better quality, there would be more engineering synergies with Ferrari, a return to the track – and, most significantly, a return to the lucrative US market Maserati had been absent from since 1990. Employees would just have to become accustomed to being part of the Ferrari family, a process which had begun when production briefly transferred to Maranello during the factory reconstruction. Among Ferrari's plans was a new, cutting-edge paint shop on its Maranello site which would set new

standards in finish for both its own cars and future Maseratis. Additionally, and somewhat controversially for purists, all engines would be designed and built by Ferrari in Maranello.

To some it was heresy but the results justified the means as sales volumes continued to expand. The 3200 GT was quickly replaced by a new model, although the open-top Spyder variant was launched first, at the Frankfurt show in 2001. The Coupé, signifying Maserati's ambitions, was launched on US soil – Detroit – the following year. Though stylistically similar to the 3200 GT it had been completely re-engineered with an emphasis on build quality, and was now powered by a dry-sumped 4.2-litre Ferrari V8 also used in the hugely popular 360 Modena.

Half a century after the last Pininfarina-bodied Maserati, the famous coachbuilder – historically associated with Ferrari – was brought in to design the bodyshell for the fifth-generation Quattroporte. Again the intention was to signal a break with the past, the fourth-generation model having sputtered out sales-wise in 2001. ItalDesign had pitched a radical idea for

ABOVE: Pininfarina styled the fifth-generation Quattroporte, establishing a new design language for future Maserati models.

OVERLEAF: Improving build quality and material feel were key targets as the company moved upmarket.

BELOW: Five metres long and two metres high, ItalDesign's Buran concept envisaged the future of limousines in MPV form.

a successor that mixed limousine and SUV elements but its concept car, the Buran – named after a Siberian wind – was considered a step too far, even with the American market in mind.

Based on the new M139 platform, powered by the same Ferrari-sourced V8 as the Coupé, and riding on adaptive suspension, the latest Quattroporte was a remarkable departure from the conservatism of previous models – and the rest of its sector. Pininfarina chief designer Ken Okuyama cleverly integrated existing design cues into a shape with a genuinely imposing presence, while introducing new ideas such as the large-format grille which would define Maseratis for years to come. Shortly after its public debut at Frankfurt in September 2003 it was shown to the high-net-worth US audience at the Pebble Beach Concours d'Elegance, a confident statement of intent by the company. Its sheer size was a clear pitch to the US market: while the fourth-generation model had been criticized

for having too small a cabin, this latest one boasted similar dimensions to the Mercedes S-Class.

ABOVE: Based on the Ferrari Enzo and bristling with advanced technology, the MC12 race car sparked outrage among racing rivals.

All this took place against a background of disarray in the wider Fiat Group following the death of Gianni Agnelli from prostate cancer in January 2003. Fiat Auto's losses were contaminating the financial health of the wider organization, and would trigger a period of tumult as corporate predators circled while the Agnelli dynasty wrestled with the matter of succession. Ultimately his chosen heir, grandson John Elkann, would win out, making the key hire of lawyer and corporate turnaround specialist Sergio Marchionne, who became Fiat Group's CEO in 2004.

For a brief period Maserati would remain largely untouched by the chaos elsewhere in the empire and continued its plans to re-enter the racing scene. Giorgio Ascanelli, race engineer to Ayrton Senna and Gerhard Berger at McLaren in Formula 1 at the turn of the 1990s, led development of what would become the MC12, based on the carbonfibre monocoque underpinnings

BELOW: Fifty road-going examples of the 217mph MC12
were built to satisfy FIA homologation requirements, half of
them 150mm shorter owing to a rule change.

of the Ferrari Enzo supercar and using its gearbox and a dry-sumped version of its V12 engine. Only the windscreen was shared with the donor car; the MC12 received a longer and wider bodyshell which was among the first works at Ferrari–Maserati of new design director Frank Stephenson, acclaimed designer of the new Mini. Although the first sketch was produced by Fabrizio Giugiaro, son of Giorgetto, and subject to aerodynamic work by Dialma Zinelli at Dallara, Stephenson was responsible for one of the most important elements of its final evolution: making it road-legal. Among the chief requirements of the programme was the ability to produce 25 road-going equivalents to satisfy the homologation requirements of its target series, the FIA GT Championship.

Nevertheless, the MC12 had a troubled journey through the homologation process as other competitors lobbied against the FIA permitting such a technically advanced car to compete. The debate continued even as the first MC12s were finally allowed to compete in the final rounds of the 2004 FIA GT season. Thereafter it became one of the most competitive cars in the series, despite being subject to various balance-of-performance handicaps to furnish a more level playing field.

At the MC12's first 'shakedown' run at Ferrari's Fiorano test track in early 2004, the nearby factory practically emptied as staff rushed to see the new car in action: F1 team boss Jean Todt and world champion Michael Schumacher watched as Andrea Bertolini conducted its first lap. It then spent three hours in the garage while a broken driveshaft was fixed, but this was probably a positive in terms of Maranello productivity.

The operational intimacy between Ferrari and Maserati, unthinkable in the earlier years of the two companies, had set the trident marque on the road back to greatness – but a fork in that road was now approaching. As the Fiat Group restructured under Sergio Marchionne, with a view to ultimately splitting Ferrari off and floating it on the stock exchange, Maserati – still making a paper loss – had to be removed from Maranello's balance sheet. The companies were separated in April 2005 and Maserati became part of the Fiat Group once again.

"I believe very much in Maserati," said Marchionne at the time, "but Maserati must believe in itself."

To the
Second Century

Sharing and Electrifying

When Sergio Marchionne, already CEO of the Fiat Group, replaced Herbert Demel as CEO of Fiat Auto in February 2005 it signified a major shift in direction for the troubled car maker – and the other manufacturers in the empire. Demel, the first non-Italian to head up Fiat, had been brought in just 18 months earlier with a mandate to repair relations with General Motors; a 'strategic partnership' between the two entities had soured when Fiat's previous leadership had sought to resolve their financial problems by triggering a contractual clause which would have forced GM to expand its 20 per cent shareholding in Fiat.

Regime change can be brutal. Within two months Marchionne had transferred Maserati from Ferrari's ownership, removed the recently appointed Martin Leach as head of Maserati and added the Modenese subsidiary to the remit of Alfa Romeo CEO Karl-Heinz Kalbfell – another newcomer to the Fiat conglomerate. After several years of intimate connection with one old track rival, Maserati would now be tied to another. The commercial realities of

OPPOSITE: Millennial Maserati cockpits were clearly Ferrari-based.

OPPOSITE: Sergio
Marchionne rescued
the Fiat Group but his
ascent to power brought
political turbulence
in its wake, including
a rotating cast of
Maserati CEOs.

car manufacture in the twenty-first century dictated more use of common parts, including entire platforms; Maserati's adoption of Ferrari powertrains (and, in the case of the MC12, much of the underlying chassis and mechanical platform) represented the first steps into this new world. How would the marque retain its identity as its centenary approached?

Although Maserati was still booking an operating loss, owing to the recent and very necessary investment in its manufacturing facilities, sales were surging. It was Alfa Romeo which was the sick man of the Fiat Group. Decades of national ownership before it fell into Fiat's orbit had virtually killed the brand, as lackadaisical build quality and poor materials undid the appeal of quirky designs. Marchionne's vision was to relaunch it as an upmarket sporting brand, albeit at a price point some way south of Maserati.

On paper, Kalbfell was the ideal figure to oversee this brand transformation while continuing to nurture Maserati's return to health. A BMW man since 1977, he combined engineering savvy with a clear idea of product: Kalbfell had been instrumental in BMW's return to Formula 1 and superintended the rebirth of the Mini and Rolls-Royce brands under BMW ownership. But as a hire of the previous regime – headhunted by Demel – he would likely be on borrowed time in a period of corporate bloodletting under a new overall boss. It came to pass with startling rapidity. Just months after laying out his vision for Maserati – "Its relationship with Ferrari will continue, and it'll continue to build beautiful, individual, exclusive Italian cars" he told the *Telegraph* newspaper – he was effectively demoted, remaining CEO of Maserati alone as Antonio Baravalle was put in charge of Alfa Romeo. Life in the boardroom of Italy's biggest industrial group must have resembled an episode of *Game of Thrones*.

When Kalbfell arrived, development of a replacement for the 4200 Coupé and its Spyder variant was well underway. But the new sales target of 10,000 units per year (almost double what Maserati actually sold in 2005) prompted a change in priorities, as it became clear the new model would be more expensive to manufacture. Ferrari gratefully took on the project – it eventually became the F149 California – and Maserati pivoted to a new concept. Given the chosen launch date of the 2007 Geneva Show, the clock was ticking. Maserati had less than a year to design, develop and tool up for production – hence the decision to base the Coupé's replacement on a shortened version of the M139 platform which underpinned the Quattroporte.

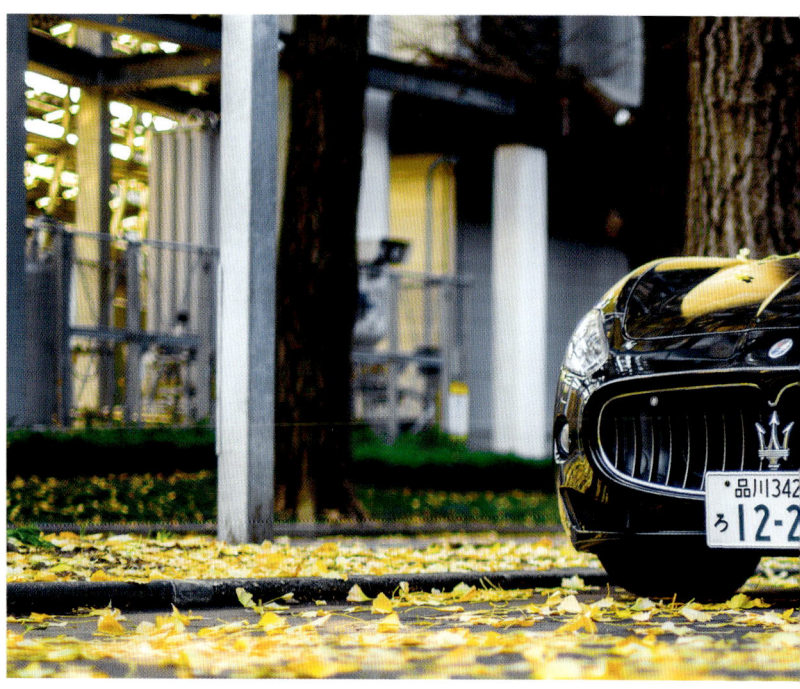

At the time, industry insiders speculated that the cost-cutting measures would extend to Maserati dropping the V8 engine in favour of a 3.2-litre Alfa Romeo V6 originally developed by General Motors. Brand loyalists were therefore delighted when the new car, named the GranTurismo, was unveiled – not only did the muscular, purposeful shell (styled by one of Pininfarina's new stars, Jason Castriota) feature a grille which harked back to the A6GCS, under the bonnet the 4.2-litre V8 remained in place. Castriota had been involved in Pininfarina's Birdcage 75th, an MC12-based concept shown at Geneva in 2005 to mark the coachbuilder's 75th anniversary, and the lines of that car – which itself aped the Birdcage

Maseratis of the 1960s – were reflected in the flowing lines of the GranTurismo's front wings.

Response in the media was mixed, since the GranTurismo's close relationship with the Quattroporte made it heavier and less agile than some rival cars. Writing in *Car* magazine, the comic actor and sportscar aficionado Rowan Atkinson summed up the GranTurismo's ethos: "If you were expecting a hardcore driver's coupé, this isn't it. But it was always Maserati's intention to make this car biased more towards luxury than performance: 40 per cent are US-bound, after all. And enthusiasts at least have the comfort of knowing that more focused versions will come later."

Maserati had signalled the arrival of a more performance-oriented option and that hit the market a year later, packing a 4.9-litre V8 with a six-speed Graziano automated manual gearbox. A racing version, the MC, followed in 2009 with a specific mandate for competition in the FIA GT4 series.

While it was known that Maserati was also evaluating a launch into the SUV segment – one which accounted for a substantial element of the US market and which was increasingly popular in the US – it would not happen on Kalbfell's watch. In September 2006 he abruptly departed, replaced by Fiat's head of fleet car sales, Roberto Ronchi. The cycle of executive churn continued as Ronchi enjoyed just under two years in the hot seat before making way for Harald Wester, who dovetailed this role with his existing one of Chief Technical Officer for the entire Fiat Group.

Regardless of developments in the boardroom, in 2007 Maserati had made a profit for the first time since Fiat had acquired it from De Tomaso. Sales of 7,496 units, driven by strong European demand for the Quattroporte and GranTurismo, were a new record even if they fell short of the 10,000 target announced in 2005. Under Wester, Maserati

ABOVE: The sixth Quattroporte completed Maserati's transition to in-house styling and was built in the newly refitted ex-Bertone Grugliasco plant near Turin.

BELOW: Based on Jeep Cherokee mechanicals, the Kubang show car was an exercise in seeing if the world was ready for a Maserati SUV.

would take more steps towards the mainstream, revealing the Kubang concept car at the 2011 Frankfurt Show. The name was an explicit throwback to an earlier Giugiaro-designed concept shown at Detroit eight years previously and based on the mechanicals of an Audi A8. That car, the Kubang GT, was a putative co-production with Audi which fell through the cracks in the dog days of the De Tomaso ownership. Though the 2011 Kubang was described as an evolution of that concept it had practically nothing in common with it, based as it was on the Jeep Cherokee platform but powered by the familiar Ferrari-Maserati V8. Here the world got its first glimpse of what a Maserati SUV would look like.

Wester's stated aim was to have a range of six models and reach 70,000 worldwide sales by 2018. An ambitious target but achievable through the adoption of a new rear-wheel-drive

platform, codenamed M156, which would underpin the next generation of Maseratis as well as achieving cost amortization through deployment elsewhere in a Fiat empire which was, against expectations, growing.

Maserati was not the only company in the Fiat Group which had become profitable. In 2009 Sergio Marchionne had achieved the seemingly impossible and returned Fiat Auto's balance sheet to the black. His ambition did not stop there. Across the Atlantic, the Chrysler Group was in dire peril and Marchionne offered the hand of partnership – one which, through a complicated process of financial engineering which involved Chrysler filing for Chapter 11 bankruptcy protection, and the tacit assistance of the Barack Obama administration, would lead to the formation of Fiat Chrysler Automobiles five years later, in 2014.

The partnership and gradual merging of the two enterprises would enable the M156 platform to underpin new Chrysler

ABOVE: Although the Kubang was shown in 2011, it would be another five years until the first Maserati SUV entered showrooms. Though anathema to sportscar purists, this segment is a must for all mainstream car makers.

models and provide a new engine option for Maserati in the form of Chrysler's Pentastar V6. A twin-turbo three-litre V6 based on the Pentastar was the entry-level engine in the fifth-generation Quattroporte, introduced in 2013 and based on the M156. In the same year Maserati revived the Ghibli name in a new mid-size luxury saloon based on a shortened M156 platform. Both cars were built in a new factory near Milan, formerly owned by Bertone.

Wester handed over to new CEO Reid Bigland in 2016, having expanded sales to over 36,000 units per year. Among his last acts was to unveil the Levante, the definitive Maserati SUV, named after the easterly wind that blows through the Strait of Gibraltar. Purists, naturally, were aghast – there was a diesel engine option, too. But this was not the most significant development in the Italian car industry that year: in January Marchionne announced that Ferrari would be split

off from the larger group and floated on the New York Stock Exchange to bankroll a larger investment programme across FCA. As part of this Ferrari would ultimately cease to supply engines to Maserati.

In the summer of 2018 Marchionne unexpectedly resigned from all his positions within Fiat Chrysler Automobiles. On 25 July he died. It subsequently emerged he had been treated for cancer for over a year. Naturally the immense power vacuum created by his absence led to further boardroom tumult and Maserati would have two more CEOs – Tim Kuniskis and Davide Grasso – before FCA merged with Peugeot–Citroën to form the Stellantis Group in 2021. After decades apart, Maserati and Citroën would enjoy family ties again.

In 2022, Maserati returned to single-seater competition 65 years after Adolfo Orsi reluctantly closed the company's factory racing team. This, at least, was the marketing gloss. The reality was somewhat more nuanced: Maserati entered a naming and powertrain partnership in Formula E, the FIA's top-level electric racing championship, with the Monaco-based MSG team which had previously run under the Venturi banner. Thus it was more akin to Maserati's brief late-1960s reappearance as an engine supplier to Cooper.

Formula E has proven itself as a technology incubator as well as a focus for marketing high-performance electric vehicles. In its first year it was purely a branding exercise since the cars and powertrains were standardized but, while the chassis and batteries remain identical, manufacturers have been able to construct their own electric motors and gearboxes since the second season. Maserati's arrival coincided with the debut of the third-generation FE car, featuring four-wheel drive and capable of reaching 200mph. The deal with MSG not only enabled Maserati to have title

OPPOSITE: While Formula E is largely a branding exercise, it offers Maserati a marketing platform for its bold plans to go all-electric by 2030.

BELOW: The MC20 two-seat sportscar introduced the company's last internal combustion engine, a twin-spark V6 related to the one used in the Alfa Romeo Stelvio.

ABOVE: The Grecale SUV slotted in below the Levante in the range and is assembled alongside its Alfa Romeo Stelvio sibling at the Stellantis-owned Cassino plant.

branding for the entire project, it also enabled it to badge the car the Tipo Folgore, a moniker which combined an antique Maserati naming convention with the new title for the company's electric road car offerings.

Folgore – Italian for a bolt of lightning – would distinguish the all-electric models from their petrol-powered brethren. In 2023 Maserati unveiled the Grecale, a new small SUV which slotted in under the Levante, initially with a turbocharged inline-four engine in a choice of two power outputs, plus a performance-oriented Trofeo model.

For the 2024 model year it added a fully electric Folgore model alongside a new GranTurismo with a twin-turbo V6, plus a Folgore-badged variant in which three electric motors combined to deliver the equivalent of 818bhp to all four wheels. Capable of accelerating from rest to 60mph in a claimed 2.7 seconds, the GranTurismo Folgore comprehensively outperformed its conventional counterparts, the most powerful of which mustered 542bhp.

While keen drivers may struggle to adjust to the absence of the familiar sounds of internal combustion, high-end performance cars can mitigate this through responsiveness and brutal acceleration. In the GranTurismo Folgore one motor drives the front axle while the other two individually drive the rear wheels, allowing for a torque-vectoring feature claimed to replicate the characteristics of a limited-slip differential.

These new models were acting as a symbolic passing of the baton. In line with the policy of the rest of the Stellantis Group, Maserati announced another significant development for the company: the gradual phasing out of pure-internal combustion powertrains from the 2025 model year onwards and a commitment to going all-electric in 2030. The arrival of the first electric powertrains in the GranTurismo and Grecale would dovetail with the end of production of the twin-turbo V8.

Electrification represents a problematic necessity for every performance car manufacturer except those vanishing few who enjoy a client base for whom money is no object. But the fact is fossil fuels are running out and synthetic fuels are yet to be produced at scale. Maserati's bold plunge into total electrification is an unusual move in this space, but not at all out of character for a marque which has gone to the edge of extinction more than once and survived – and thrived.

INDEX

(Key: *italic* refers to photos/captions)